Success Through Subconscious Mastery

Achieve Your Dreams by Integrating the Power of Hypnotherapy into Your Everyday Life

By
Ausra Cerniauskiene, CHt

Disclaimer

While Ausra Cerniauskiene has made a concerted, conscientious effort to provide accurate information at the time of publishing, she does not claim that all information provided is entirely correct and current. Readers should always practice due diligence and research credible primary sources before relying on such information. Furthermore, the author does not by any means assert the ability to provide medical, psychological, or health-related advice to any individuals.

This publication's goal is to provide valuable information for readers that will inspire them to pursue their own study of the topic. It is not meant as a substitute for expert help and support. If you require such a level of assistance, please seek the services of a competent professional.

Details of client cases have been fictionalized and their names have been changed in an effort to preserve the meaning and significance of each story while fully protecting client privacy.

© 2021 All Rights Reserved

Foreword

I have known Ausra for almost a decade. When I first met her, I was drawn to her kindness and genuine interest in others. Ausra is a thinker, and her gentle, inquisitive nature is quite disarming, so you feel comfortable and validated in her presence. As a thinker, Ausra has never been one to simply accept the way things are; rather, she always wants to know why things are. In fact, asking "why" set Ausra on the path to discover why some people stay stuck and others thrive. This is a great question that many of us have probably pondered ourselves—I know I have. In her quest to unlock this mystery, Ausra became fascinated with hypnotherapy, and it emerged as her true calling. Now, she has joined the select few who can be classified as "thrivers." Luckily for us, Ausra has graciously put her discoveries to pen and paper, so we can all benefit from what she has uncovered, implemented, and integrated into her own life, which has flourished as a result.

As it turns out, we all have the potential to become "thrivers." The secret to unlocking this potential lies in our minds and the way we think. Most of our thought processes are unconscious; we plod along on autopilot, doing what we do but never feeling content. Many of us feel stuck and helpless. We don't know how to change, so we end up repeating tired patterns, which means that a new job, new friends, or a new living space only offer momentary, fleeting happiness, instead of long-lasting fulfillment. After the initial rush of newness, we slip back into our old mental ruts that leave us feeling sad, tired, and unsure. What if you discovered that it doesn't have to be this way? What if you discovered a way to shape-shift your life into something that brings you peace, wholeness, and satisfaction? What if you realized that the power is actually in you, the way Dorothy discovered she had the power within herself all along to go where she wanted to be in The Wizard of Oz? She needed no wizard (or anything external) to make her dream come true, and neither do you.

The first step in shape-shifting your life is to ask, "Why?" Just like it was for Ausra, this question is the first step in unraveling the years of unconscious thinking patterns that have created your present state. When you ask "why," you begin to see. Once you see, you can understand, and once you understand, you can change.

For those who want to end a negative habit, get out of a rut, or reach a goal that has always seemed unattainable, you will need to become a mental detective of sorts. The process of becoming a master thinker will help you to see the ultimate reasons you have been stuck.

The power of positive thinking isn't a new concept, but simple as it may be in theory, putting it into practice and sustaining it is initially challenging for most of us. However, once you start to connect the dots and your mental patterns are exposed, the payoff will lead to incredible freedom. Discovering that YOU have been the driver of your life all the while is a monumental revelation. Once that shift happens, you will forever be changed, and your view of yourself will become your superpower!

Francesca Cappucci

Actress and Screenwriter

Table of Contents

Introduction 1

CHAPTER 1 5

Power Revealed 5

My Journey 9

Meet Yourself Wherever You Are 12

You Aren't the Problem, but Your Approach
Might Be 13

It's All about Alignment 17

Access the Subconscious 21

Knowing Better vs. Doing Better 25

The Goal of Your Subconscious Mind 26

The Comfort of the Struggle 33

The Benefit of Staying Stuck 36

CHAPTER 2 38

Real vs. Imaginary 38

See It Before It Manifests 40

When You Think You Can't Visualize 44

Seeing vs. Knowing 46

Act As If 48
Feel the Feelings 49
Harness Your Sense of Hearing 51
A Sense of Knowing 53
Understanding Intuition 56
Past Projections 59
Wishful Thinking 61
Trust Your Intuition… Sometimes 62
Future Decision Making 64

CHAPTER 3 67
Bring About Positive Change 67
Strengthen Awareness 73
Hypnotherapy 75
Self-Hypnosis 80
Affirmations 83
Questions for the Subconscious 87

CHAPTER 4 92
Your Story 92
The Patterns in Other People's Lives 95
Acknowledge the Existing Narrative 102
Become an Outside Observer 103
Choose Your Next Adventure 106

CHAPTER 5 111
Dive Deeper 111

Past, Present, Future	112
Understanding Your Memory	115
Memory Retrieval	117
Memory Malleability	120
A Positive Perception of the Past	123
Memory Reconstruction	128
Avoid Distorted Memories	133
Dream Therapy	135
Dream Stages	139
Remember Your Dreams	140
Dream Analysis Process	141
Self Mastery	148

Introduction

Some moments in life change everything. They set the stage for our next chapter—a chapter full of growth, goals achieved, and dreams reached. These moments take everything we thought we were sure of—what we thought we knew for certain—and flip it upside down. They completely change our perspective. We watch as what we thought we knew goes up in flames. Then, we're left to recalibrate, recreate, and rebuild ... often from the ground up. In these moments, our beliefs and outlook on life are forever changed. They mark the start of our next phase in life; from this point forward, we measure time in terms of 'before this' and 'after this.'

Most of the time, you'll never see it coming. The moments that change everything seem to happen when you least expect it. Maybe it's a chance encounter, a sudden tragedy, a promotion, or a breaking point when you have nothing left to give and yell up to the sky, "Enough is enough!"

While Hollywood can make it seem like experiencing a big event is an essential jumping-off point that acts as a catalyst to move you towards your next chapter, that's not always the case. The benefit of that realization is that you understand you don't need a major plot twist in your life to change your life. You don't have to wait until you get laid off from your job, get the marriage proposal, or experience any other major life event, good or bad. You don't have to sit idly by, waiting for the next big milestone to start your next chapter. Your next chapter can start when you simply decide it's time. That power resides within you. This book will provide you with the tools and understanding to bring that power to life and step into your next chapter.

If you hope to change your life and get to the next level, you're in the right place. In this book's following chapters, I will remind you of what's possible for you and show you how much closer you are to living your dreams than you probably realize. I'll share personal insights, stories, and client results (all of whom have given me permission to share their journey) that will reveal the truth. You've had the power within you all along. I'm looking forward to guiding you through this journey, and I can't wait to show you how to use your inherent wisdom to achieve all of your desires.

If you're unsure about all of these claims, I don't blame you in the slightest. If you are skeptical, that's understandable. In fact, I expect it. This book may be one of many personal development books you own because you strive to be your best on a regular basis. You might have purchased it on a whim, in hopes of changing your life once and for all. Regardless of the reason(s) you're reading this book or your level of skepticism, I'm glad you're here, and I want you to know that change is possible.

Please bear a few things in mind as you read through this book. As you delve deeper and learn how to tap into the power of your inner mind, you will be introduced to several new exercises and practices that will aid in your progress towards your goals. With that being said, I highly suggest you give each one of these tasks a chance, even if some of them seem illogical on the surface or too simple to be effective. I have strategically selected the exercises and practices within this book to support you in your self-development. I have seen firsthand how they can foster substantial growth and change. So, even if you don't think you'll benefit from a specific exercise, I recommend you give it a shot, rather than pushing it to the back burner or dismissing it out of hand.

Additionally, I want you to know I'm not trying to convince you of anything—that's not what this book is about. I'm simply sharing my own experiences and the inner workings of the mind as I've come to understand them through my training and life experiences. You can use the same insight to achieve your goals and bring your dreams to life.

The possibility of leading a meaningful life is within reach for everyone, and this promise applies to you, as well. This book will inspire you while equipping you with the tools to overcome challenges that prevent you from living your best life. Let's dive in!

CHAPTER 1
Power Revealed

"The only person you are destined to become is the person you decide to be."

- Ralph Waldo Emerson

For most of my adult life, I felt like I was merely going through the motions. I was doing all the things I was supposed to do, and from an outsider's perspective, I was successful. Sure, I experienced highs and lows and moments in between when I was certain my future was bleak, but those moments were fleeting. All in all, my life was good. Even so, I couldn't seem to shake the ever-looming feeling that something was missing, although I wasn't exactly sure what it was.

I didn't know if everyone felt this same lingering emotion or if I was alone in my longing for more. I'd watch my friends and family go through challenging times and struggle with a variety of issues that life seemed to throw their way. They'd often come out on the other side and would eventually reach their goals. I started to notice a pattern that led me to wonder if some of their struggles were self-inflicted, unbeknownst to them. In certain cases, it appeared like their struggle came right before their breakthrough.

I witnessed a friend of mine, Sandra, go through a powerful example of this phenomenon. Sandra was normally a direct, straightforward woman who knew exactly what she wanted, so I was surprised to notice a shift in her behavior years ago, during one of our lunch dates. At this point, I had started to recognize some sort of correlation between struggle and success among some of my friends, but I didn't have a real handle on it. I was aware of a pattern, but I wasn't sure if it was significant. However, when Sandra rushed into the cafe where we were meeting and started questioning everything she was doing, from the food she ordered to whether she should take a call when her phone rang, I knew something was up. I didn't say anything about it at first, but as I watched my normally collected, direct, and decisive (about literally everything) friend act like a different person, I knew I had to speak up. Halfway through our lunch, I asked her if she was okay, but even then I didn't get a straight answer.

At that point I was not a hypnotherapist, but Sandra's sudden burst of self-doubt was deeply concerning, so I did the only thing I knew to do: I became curious. I asked her what I thought were simple, open-ended questions that didn't require her to make any decisions but instead simply allowed her to express herself, and I made suggestions here and there.

Looking back, I now realize that I was using hypnotherapy and focus-shifting techniques without even realizing it. Sure enough, the truth was revealed. She had recently received an email from a tech company she had dreamed of working with for as long as I had known her. She was on the verge of everything she ever wanted, but at some level she felt undeserving. It seemed as if a part of her wanted to have to fight tirelessly and struggle before she would feel worthy of working with this company that she idealized. Knowing what I know now, it's clear to me she was unintentionally self-sabotaging.

That experience with Sandra solidified my belief that struggle and breakthrough are often connected. Isn't it funny how much easier it is to observe patterns within those you love than it is to see the same patterns within yourself?

I had to know more about the correlation between struggle and success. Did the emotional turmoil my friend went through serve a purpose? Was it necessary? Did she believe on some level that she was only worthy of her aspirations after she proved she could conquer her challenges? If that hypothesis was true, then maybe the struggle I felt about believing more was "out there for me" wasn't required. Maybe I could change my mind, have my breakthrough, and manifest my desires without the struggle.

My struggle was different from Sandra's, but it was still very valid. I grappled with the feeling that I was meant for more, but the clear direction I was hoping for wasn't showing up in the timely manner I wanted. I believe many of us feel this way to some extent. We spend so much time subconsciously making things harder for ourselves that we end up consciously fixating on our goals. We make little to no progress forward. We go through the motions, often struggling every step of the way. Then we end up waiting for our big break to reach out and tap us on the shoulder, but it doesn't. Somewhere in that waiting period, we get frustrated and confused.

When we have dreams, goals, and aspirations that we don't fully and completely believe we can achieve, we put a lot of pressure on our timeline. We want it right now because at some level (most likely the subconscious level) we're not convinced it's on its way to us. However, when we know it's already ours, and its manifestation in physical form is just a matter of time and acceptance, then we can embrace where we are in the current moment without self-doubt or self-imposed pressure.

Now, I did not used to believe I could accomplish

all my goals. I certainly didn't believe that everyone else could accomplish theirs, either. I thought that type of success was reserved for a few lucky people. But through a series of life events, I came to realize that the desires of my heart were there for a reason, and even more importantly, they were within reach.

Whether you know exactly what you want and can see it so vividly that it feels as if it's right in front of you, or you know you're meant to accomplish big things in this world but your dreams aren't as tangible, I want you to know you can find a path toward all your goals. The best part is that the secrets to achieving them are already within you at this very moment—they have always been and will always be. It's simply a matter of realizing the power you have within your subconscious mind and using it to fuel your desires and propel you toward everything you've ever wanted.

My Journey

The power of my subconscious mind was revealed to me during a pretty mundane period in my life. I had been lost for what seemed like an incredibly long time. I was going through the motions, working a job that didn't light me up inside, and tackling life as it came. My life wasn't bad, but it wasn't the fulfilling existence I had envisioned for myself at a young age. I always had a feeling that more was out there for me, although I couldn't pinpoint what it was exactly. As the years went by, I eventually got to the point where I felt like I had no other choice but to face reality: I wasn't living the meaningful life I had always longed for, and I lacked the clarity I needed to progress forward. No matter what my next step was, though, I knew I wasn't going to settle for a "good-enough" life—I was determined to make it extraordinary.

Contrary to how it might seem, it is possible to accept what's showing up for you in the present moment and to continue planning for the future, which is exactly what I did. Although I didn't know what my true purpose was at the time, I knew I needed some sort of guidance to get where I wanted to go. My job didn't inspire and fulfill me, so I decided to start there. I took a career counseling course, intending to be matched with a career that would lead to fulfillment. Much to my (and my instructor's) surprise, out of thousands of potential occupations, the closest fit for me was just over a 50% match. Naturally, I was disheartened. I thought that if I sought out a structured path with guidance from a career course, I'd have my answer to fulfillment in no time, but it was becoming more and more evident that was not the case.

The conventional route was clearly not providing

me with any answers, so I dove into the law of attraction and spirituality, which eventually led me to a shaman. He provided me with homework rituals and guidance, and within a few weeks, I stumbled upon hypnotherapy. The concept of hypnotherapy wasn't something I was familiar with at the time, but the power of the subconscious mind was something in which I had always been interested. The more I learned about it, the more my hunch was confirmed. Hypnotherapy was, in fact, my true calling.

Through my extensive training, education, and life experiences that led me to become a hypnotherapist, I learned how to use my subconscious mind to achieve my goals. I regularly manifest things that once seemed completely out of reach. My life was transformed in countless ways, and I owe those changes to my ability to understand the mind and hypnotherapy. Just as important, I'm able to empower my clients across the world to break through mental barriers that keep them from thriving in all areas of their lives.

A small part of me wishes I had some thrilling story to share about how my path to fulfillment and purpose appeared on an enormous sign with flashing red lights and arrows that read, "This is the answer you've been looking for!" However, I know that's not how life works most of the time. Far too often, I see people get stuck because they're waiting for definitive direction from an outside source. Through my own personal development journey and my work with a shaman, among other things, I was able to develop my "inner knowing" (more on this concept later). My inner knowing was just as powerful, if not more powerful, than any tangible confirmation I could have possibly received. But if I were to accredit my deep sense of knowing to one factor, it would be my thorough understanding of the subconscious mind. Inner knowing is one more reason to learn how to harness the power of your inner mind to work in your favor.

I share this personal journey to remind you that you don't need some enormous breakthrough or life-altering moment to change your life. Taking aligned action and using the skills you already have within (which we'll uncover throughout this book) is more than enough.

Meet Yourself Wherever You Are

Your inner wisdom is constantly working behind the scenes to keep you safe. So, it's important to acknowledge that at this moment, you're right where you're meant to be, and your inner mind (your subconscious mind) is doing an incredible job. You're not doing it "wrong," and your feelings are completely valid, whatever they may be. I want you to remember this point as you move forward.

As you open the door to your subconscious and gain an understanding of your true power (the power you've always had), there's no point in beating yourself up about where you are right now in your journey because it led you here. This place is where you will learn that you have the power to create the reality you want at any given moment.

You Aren't the Problem, but Your Approach Might Be

Up until this point, you've likely been trying to achieve your goals through sheer willpower and motivation alone. If you're not sure whether this statement is true for you, here are some common examples of doing so:

- You allow excuses that delay your progress. For instance, you tell yourself you're too busy to take action, but when you do have free time, you find yourself searching for other excuses that keep you stuck.
- You feel like accomplishing your goals is always an uphill battle. Nothing flows. You find very little joy in the journey.
- You show up inconsistently, despite how hard you try to stay disciplined.

Above all else, the biggest telltale sign that you're relying solely on willpower and motivation is that you don't take action toward your goals when you're lacking the energy or you're not in the mood. Even the most dedicated individuals have days when they lack the stamina and drive to push through with brute force alone. It's bound to happen at some point because you're human, and there's simply no way to maintain 100% self-control and drive all the time.

If you can relate to this, then I suspect your journey to achieve your goals has not been a smooth and steady one. You may blame yourself and think you just don't have the willpower you used to or that you can't stay motivated despite your constant attempts and best effort. You probably think you have to figure out how to get and stay motivated or have better self-control to achieve your goals.

However, the reality is that you're not lacking motivation or willpower. It's just that your level of motivation and willpower fluctuates, as everyone's does. Even if you can't remember the last time you felt motivated to take action or had the willpower to do so, it's likely because you burned yourself out from trying so hard to make progress, while you unknowingly took the wrong approach.

Whatever the case may be, I assure you that your motivation and willpower are not the actual issues. The real problem is that you're essentially assigning the task of goal achievement to your willpower and motivation, which is far beyond the scope of what they can accomplish. So blaming a lack of progress on either of those things doesn't make much sense.

Willpower and motivation alone are not enough. Think about it this way: Imagine trying to reach the top of a mountain, and being stubbornly committed to getting there on a bicycle with two tires that are slowly losing air. Can you eventually make it up the mountain? Sure, it's possible. Will you eventually make it up the mountain? Maybe. Maybe not. If you do, it's going to be a nightmare of an experience with a lot of stops in between. But let's say you do eventually make it to the top. You very likely won't be able to enjoy the view because you'll be completely emotionally, physically, and mentally drained from the journey. I have to ask: If the journey is such a challenge that you wonder whether reaching the destination was even worth it, what is the point?

Similarly, operating solely through your conscious mind (the part of your mind where willpower and motivation are stored, along with logical thinking) can certainly work. But just like making your way uphill on a bike with two deflating tires, it's extraordinarily difficult and tiresome.

Fortunately, another part of your mind is far more powerful and a much better fit to help you achieve your goals. I'm referring to your subconscious mind, or as I sometimes call it, the inner mind. When you tap into the power of your subconscious mind to make progress toward your goals, you streamline your path to success. Discovering your ability to use this part of your mind to create the life you want is like realizing you had the keys to your car in your pocket the entire time you were struggling to reach the mountain peak on a bicycle. You had access to an easier way to reach your destination all along. You could have driven and saved yourself much time, stress, and energy.

Remember when I said the problem with relying on motivation and willpower to achieve your goal is that they're not equipped to do the job? Well, your subconscious mind is capable of handling the task. Your subconscious is where your long-term memories, habits, beliefs, and emotions (among other things) are stored. By going directly to the source, you can remove the blocks that hold you back from achieving your goals by neutralizing traumatic events that hold you back from living your best life, breaking habits, and/or overcoming barriers that keep you stagnant (like writer's block, for instance). You can literally transform your reality.

It's All about Alignment

If the conscious and the subconscious mind were in a tug-of-war, the subconscious mind would win every single time. It's far more powerful than the conscious mind, which is why it's imperative to align it with the goals you're trying to achieve. Otherwise, you'll always find yourself getting one step ahead, only to wind up two steps back. When your conscious desires are in alignment with your subconscious beliefs and habits, you can't be stopped.

Everyone who walks into my hypnotherapy office has some sort of underlying struggle between what they want on a conscious level and what their subconscious mind has programmed or deemed as 'safe.' However, this ongoing internal battle isn't reserved only for those who can't stop smoking or have a fear of flying. It's safe to say that this is a struggle we've all faced in one way or another, at some point in time.

I recently saw a client (we'll call her Mary), who is an outstanding example of what happens when someone's conscious goals and subconscious beliefs are in conflict and how getting them on the same page can make all the difference. Mary booked her hypnotherapy appointment with the goal of overcoming her constant tardiness. Even as a child, she believed something would always get in her way and prevent her from arriving on time. So guess what happened? She proved herself right—she was always late. The Universe (or some all-powerful being) wasn't conspiring against her, though. Rather, her belief that she was always late overrode her conscious desire to be on time. Regardless of whether she planned to arrive at her destination right on time or half an hour early, it didn't make any difference. She would unintentionally get in her own way.

So naturally, it was no surprise when she arrived at my office 20 minutes late. I vividly remember a moment during her intake when she leaned over the arm of her chair to get closer to me and sheepishly whispered, "I can't help but feel like I'm blocking my own progress. I know the right actions to take to arrive on time, but I just don't do them, and I have no idea why. Or I start to take the right steps, and then I get sidetracked just long enough to ensure that I will be tardy."

Mary also told me that sometimes she would catch herself getting distracted right before she was supposed to leave her house. On other occasions, she would leave her house on time, but she noticed she would subconsciously manifest issues on the way to her destination. Fortunately for Mary, she was very self-aware; she was cognizant of the fact that she was getting in her own way, which constantly resulted in her being late for every important event in her life. She just didn't know why she was stuck in this cycle or how to break it.

I could see she was obviously embarrassed and wanted to change. It also became clear the results of her efforts, up until that point, had been stagnant. Whether she put 100% of her focus toward arriving on time or made no attempt at all seemed to make very little difference. She had been trying to resolve this issue on her own for so long without success that she felt she had nearly exhausted all her options, and hypnotherapy was her last shot.

A lack of progress is an all-too-common outcome that many people face, especially when they try to strong-arm their way through a problem on a conscious level. They find themselves at a standstill because their underlying subconscious belief is their main issue. Mary's conscious desire to arrive on time wasn't her problem. She already knew the devastating impact of being late for everything. Throughout her life, she had missed several job interviews because of her tardiness. She was even late for her own brother's wedding. What really upset her was when people in her life started making attempts to work around her tardiness and adjust their own lives to accommodate her because she evidently wasn't going to change. She began to notice that when her friends would invite her to a function, they would tell her the event started an hour before it really did. Once she even found an invitation to a girlfriend's dinner party that said it started at 7:00 p.m., yet she was told to arrive at 6:00 p.m. Of course, she was devastated. She felt like a little kid who needed to be given special instructions to show up on time.

Mary's issue wasn't unfixable. She was simply trying to change by using the ineffective approach of addressing only her conscious mind. In doing so, her subconscious mind remained firmly planted in the belief that she would always be late.

I immediately knew one of our goals would be to shift her belief from, "No matter what I do, I'm always late," to "I instinctually arrive on time." Through hypnotherapy, Mary aligned her subconscious mind with her conscious mind. By dismantling her old subconscious belief and reprogramming it to accept that she was capable of being on time and would be on time, she broke free from the vicious cycle of chronic tardiness. Within a very short period of just two sessions, Mary had achieved her goal. Not only did she show up to her second session with me on time, but she also revealed that she had been on time for every single appointment since our first session. She was able to finally step into the role of the dependable person she had always wanted to be.

Once Mary's subconscious belief shifted to one that supported her desire to be on time, her progress was inevitable. So, the burning question is, how do you access the subconscious mind to reach your goals?

Access the Subconscious

Have you ever had a problem or habit you wanted to change, but despite your constant attempts, you made little to no progress in the right direction? The reason for that result is probably because you were trying to make these changes without the full support of your subconscious mind.

To put this concept into perspective, let me share a helpful representation of your conscious and subconscious mind working out of alignment. Picture your subconscious mind as a pole that's cemented in the ground and your conscious mind as a rope that's lassoed around it. You're at the other end of the rope, trying to pull your subconscious beliefs toward the direction of your conscious desires. It's safe to say that won't be an easy task. Try as you might, that pole isn't going to lift out of the cement just merely because you're pulling on the rope with all of your strength. You're not going to make much progress, if any at all. You're just going to stay stuck while continuing to deplete your energy. Eventually, a point may come when you give up entirely.

This futile battle is what it's like when you try to carry out your conscious desires without your subconscious beliefs and habits being on the same page. When you access the subconscious mind, however, and change the belief associated with your goal, it's as if the cement beneath the pole dissolves and the pole itself becomes weightless. Suddenly, reaching your goal becomes a feasible and achievable outcome, which is exactly why you must align your conscious and subconscious mind to effect true and lasting change.

The first step in aligning your conscious and subconscious mind is to open and reach the subconscious mind. In order to achieve that feat, you need to do the opposite of what you do to access the conscious mind. Whenever you want to make a conscious change, you give it your full attention and take action to reach it. For instance, if you want to eat healthier, you may consciously select more nutritious food when grocery shopping.

Alternatively, to make a subconscious change, you first need to bring your subconscious mind to the forefront, and then take action by instilling new beliefs and/or habits within it. The easiest way to bring your subconscious mind to the surface is to get into a relaxed state. Once there, you can communicate directly to your subconscious mind. This endeavor can feel extremely counterintuitive at first, but it's important to understand that your subconscious mind isn't lingering solely in the background of your life. It comes to the forefront in certain moments of your day without you even realizing it.

For instance, have you ever lost your keys somewhere

in your house? If so, chances are you searched for them to no avail, only to give up and direct your attention toward something else entirely. Of course, once you relaxed and stopped consciously focusing on the misplaced keys, you suddenly remembered where they were, right?

Have you ever wondered why this phenomenon occurs? Well, once you release the pressure you place on yourself and shift your focus, your subconscious mind has the opportunity to come to the forefront and reveal the location of the misplaced keys. It's important to note that your subconscious mind takes everything in and retains what is significant to you. It stores all of your permanent memories. So, while you might not have consciously put your keys in a specific place, your subconscious mind remembered exactly where you placed them.

Subconscious mind = memory

Another example is when you forget what you were talking about in mid-conversation. Then the moment the conversation ends, you suddenly remember what you wanted to say. This common occurrence happens because your conscious mind once again shifts focus and allows your subconscious mind to come to the surface.

One of my favorite stories that showcases this concept comes from my client, Richard. I'll never forget when Richard frantically called me to book a session because he'd lost his wedding ring. He had already spent days looking for it without success when he called. All he knew was that he took it off somewhere in his house, and he'd narrowed down the timeline of when he lost it to a two-day window. Other than those specifics, he didn't know where it could be and desperately needed to find it.

During Richard's session, once he was in a deeply relaxed state, I used a variety of subconscious-hacking tools and hypnotherapy techniques to walk him back through the timeline of when he lost his ring. Using the power of his subconscious mind, he went back to the isolated event. When he emerged from his session, he had an idea of where the ring was: on top of a specific shelf in his guest bathroom. He had no conscious recollection of placing his ring in this location, so when he left my office he was skeptically optimistic.

When he called me the next day, he was in complete disbelief that he'd found his lost ring in the exact spot he'd pinpointed during his session. He wanted to know why and how hypnotherapy worked so well, as he had no conscious awareness of taking his ring off and placing it on top of the shelf where he found it.

Truth be told, one of the reasons for his success was that prior to our session he had been spending every moment of free time searching for the ring. He had been consciously racking his brain and frantically trying to retrace his steps, and his efforts completely blocked his inner mind. His subconscious had no space to reveal where the ring was. His hypnotherapy session allowed him to relax and bring his subconscious mind to the surface. At that point, the proper prompting enabled him to gather more information, remember what he thought he had completely forgotten, and find the wedding band he thought was gone forever.

Knowing Better vs. Doing Better

I am often asked, "If changing habits and reaching goals was so easy, wouldn't everybody do it?" It's a fair question. Choosing to tap into your subconscious mind to make significant changes that alter the course of your life for the better seems like an easy decision to make. After all, once someone knows better, you would assume they would do better, right? Well, not so fast.

Although that decision makes sense from a logical perspective, as you'll soon discover, the subconscious mind doesn't operate from a place of logic. Having the knowledge to change your inner mind and using that knowledge are two very different things. So, why would someone stop themselves, either consciously or subconsciously, from utilizing this power to reach their goals, achieve their dreams, and get everything they want in life?

In order to understand this mystery, you need to take three very important considerations into account:

1. The goal of your subconscious mind
2. The comfort of the struggle
3. The benefit of staying stuck

Being aware of these three factors will help you better understand yourself and others. Perhaps more importantly, it will also help ensure that you use your newfound awareness of your subconscious mind to change your life, rather than getting stuck in the trap of knowing better but failing to do better.

The Goal of Your Subconscious Mind

Your subconscious mind has one primary goal: to keep you safe. It doesn't care if you are happy, fulfilled, or living your purpose. It would be just fine with you sitting in front of a television for eight hours a day and never leaving the house if it felt that was safe. Your joy is not its problem or concern, which sounds harsh, but it's true.

If living your purpose or achieving your goal requires stepping outside of your comfort zone in any way, your inner mind isn't going to automatically jump up from the stands and become your dreams' supportive cheerleader.

In fact, it will probably work hard to get you back in your comfort zone as fast as possible because it perceives a new experience as a potential threat to your safety. So, while your conscious mind might see an unfamiliar experience as an opportunity for a better life and overall outcome, all your subconscious mind sees is caution tape with a warning about a potential threat.

Your subconscious mind will often interpret a new experience, feeling, or behavior (no matter how positive or beneficial it is to you), as an indicator that your safety is being threatened. Because its primary job is to keep you safe, the possibility of not surviving leads your inner mind to essentially sabotage your conscious desire. In other words, you end up staying stuck even though you don't want to.

The same is true for past experiences that threatened your safety, whether your safety was truly in jeopardy or your subconscious mind simply perceived said incident as a threat. On a conscious level, this response may seem very illogical. That's because your conscious mind (where you do all your thinking and rationalizing) is based on logic, whereas your subconscious mind doesn't take logic into account when forming new beliefs and habits. It takes in information and stores it similar to the way a computer stores new data. A computer doesn't automatically make updates based on the user's wants or desires. When updates are needed, someone has to uninstall the outdated software and then install a newer, more updated version of the program. Similarly, the subconscious mind doesn't interpret information or read between the lines; it accepts what it's given at face value.

Your subconscious mind will keep your current programming (your beliefs and habits) running on autopilot, regardless of how ineffective it becomes. It will maintain this status quo until you go in and manually make updates and changes. So, you should know that if you're waiting around for your inner mind to take the initiative and make adjustments or accommodations based on outdated information (what once kept you safe doesn't work for you any longer), you're going to be waiting forever. It won't happen.

Whenever I think about people who have outgrown their subconscious beliefs, I think about my longtime family friend, Victoria. I've always thought of her as a cousin because we're close in age and grew up together. Although we aren't related by blood, she's always felt like family. After going our separate ways for a few years in our twenties, we reconnected at a mutual friends' wedding. Our friendship has never required any easing into; the moment we see each other it's as if no time has passed. So, it was no surprise that during the wedding reception she was quick to confide in me about her fear of public speaking.

As it turns out, Victoria was asked to be the bride's

maid of honor, but she couldn't get over her debilitating fear to give the traditional maid of honor speech. Victoria had been able to find ways around her fear of public speaking for the previous ten years, but she was now feeling the pressure to overcome it for the first time. She realized she couldn't show up for her friends and family, excel in her career, and be who she was truly meant to be without facing her fear head on.

At some point in Victoria's life, she had an experience that led her subconscious mind to determine that public speaking wasn't safe. At least, her inner mind interpreted the situation that way, regardless of whether it was true or not. The belief formed, and her reality began to reinforce it.

Have you ever noticed that people with firm beliefs aren't as quick as others to change their minds? I believe at least one of the reasons for that tendency is because once the subconscious mind has accepted a belief, the outside world will continue to reinforce that belief by proving it to be true time and time again.

Your beliefs dictate your reality, and your reality reflects that belief back to you in your outer world. So, you're stuck in a never-ending loop until you break free. Victoria found herself in this cycle.

At the time when Victoria's belief about public speaking was formed (and perhaps even years later), it likely served her in some way. Maybe it kept her from facing the harsh ridicule of her peers or her own self-judgment, which at the time may have felt like a fate worse than death. Yet that time had passed. Her fear of public speaking was no longer in her best interest. However, just because her belief was now outdated and no longer benefiting her on a conscious level, it wasn't going to simply vanish into the unknown, never to be seen or heard from again. It still remained a valid belief and would continue to be until she reprogrammed or replaced it with a new belief.

Often we outgrow the aspects of ourselves that no longer make sense, but we continue to hold on and take the same repetitive actions because we're stuck in that belief cycle. Victoria knew this. On a conscious level, she was well aware that she was now a woman in her early twenties who was scared of doing the very thing she needed to do to live fully: speak publicly. Holding back wasn't serving her in this stage of her life.

While her subconscious mind was trying to keep her safe, all it was really doing was keeping her stagnant. Effortlessly self-assured and well put together, Victoria felt ridiculous because her fear didn't match her personality. Had she been very shy or extremely uncomfortable with attention, it might have made more sense to her on a conscious level. Due to the discrepancy between her self-esteem and her fear, her problem was especially obvious.

Once Victoria got her subconscious mind on board with her desire to speak publicly, she could achieve anything. The next time I saw Victoria, she had not only overcome her fear but blasted through it by shifting her subconscious belief to one that served her. She was thriving in multiple areas of her life, including her career where (in a perfectly-timed coincidence) she was asked to start giving monthly speeches on behalf of her company.

The bottom line: aligning your conscious and subconscious mind is the key to success, but achieving this feat requires effort. Even when you've consciously outgrown specific beliefs, habits, and fears, you must remember that your subconscious mind will still continue to be very protective and determined to keep you safe. It is also very stubborn. Once a belief is formed, your subconscious is unlikely to change or alter that belief unless it's pushed to do so.

Not everyone is fortunate enough to see the stark contrast between their subconscious beliefs and their conscious goal, like Victoria did. A great exercise to help you begin observing the disconnect between the two is to get curious. Simply start questioning your beliefs. For instance, if you want to begin exercising more often, but you believe you hate exercise and never stick with it, you're going to struggle to remain consistent. So, rather than accepting this belief and its outcome, you can start to question it—not in a judgmental tone, but in a curious way. Consider asking yourself questions such as:

- What do I think I hate about exercise?
- Have I always felt this way? When did it start?
- Do I like anything about exercising? How do I feel before, during, and after?
- In the past when I haven't stuck with it, is it because quitting feels automatic?
- Am I consciously choosing to end my workouts earlier? Or does it feel like something more is at work?

Once you start questioning your automatic responses, you may begin to see that you're operating primarily from an outdated subconscious belief. If that's the case, you will know the reason behind it. At some point, your subconscious mind formed this belief in an effort to keep you safe. I should note that this understanding isn't required in order to get your subconscious and conscious mind into alignment. However, I've found that being able to comprehend what's going on behind the scenes makes the process of reprogramming beliefs a lot smoother, especially for those who are instinctively black-and-white thinkers and analytical by nature.

The Comfort of the Struggle

Another reason you might be resistant to aligning your conscious desires with your subconscious beliefs is that, on some level, you believe the struggle is required. While I know this idea might seem absurd at first, I want you to think about a talent you've had since you were young. I'm talking about that one thing in life that comes easily to you. Maybe it's making new friends, playing the piano, writing, or something else entirely. Chances are that at some point in your life, you didn't fully appreciate that skill.

[handwritten: What is a talent I've had since I was young?]

Too often we don't place a high value on the things we are naturally good at. The same mindset holds true for the aspects of our lives where everything flows naturally. We feel this way because from a very young age we're taught to work hard for the things we want. That is a fine belief to instill, but it ties into the idea that we have to earn our place at the table. Of course, hard work has its time and place; I'm not knocking that. But it's possible you are so accustomed to the struggle that comes from constantly having to prove yourself that it feels natural—almost like a rite of passage in some way. Working tirelessly to reach your goals may be so ingrained in you that seamlessly integrating your subconscious beliefs with your conscious desires would feel entirely too easy.

In the same way, those around us tend to glorify struggle. We've all heard the stories from older generations recalling the days when they had to walk five miles uphill in the snow to get to school. Also, the movies we watch and the books we read do the same thing. The hero always starts his journey as an underdog with countless hurdles to overcome. After struggling to the point of nearly giving up, he comes out on top as the victor.

Of course, some of the trials and tribulations of life are unavoidable, but because the struggle is ingrained within us, we often struggle far more than we have to. In reality, the battle isn't always required. You may be unsure of whether you fall into the category of finding comfort in the struggle. Or, you may wonder if you unintentionally equate effort with struggle, although they are not one and the same.

If so, I'm providing the following journal prompts for you to use as a starting point to gain clarity around your potential resistance to an easier, smoother path.

- How has the struggle benefited me in the past?
- Is the struggle truly serving me at this stage in my life? If so, how? If not, why am I hanging on?
- What have I learned in the past by pushing through the struggle?
- Why do I believe that I have to prove myself through hardship?

Keep in mind that if you do uncover that you are in some way committed to the struggle, you'll get no benefit from shaming or judging yourself harshly. Any sort of newfound awareness will help you with your next breakthrough.

Now, you may be wondering, who would choose the harder path willingly? Remember, the subconscious mind doesn't operate from a place of logic. Additionally, its overall goal is to keep you safe, and it's quite unadventurous. Therefore, if the struggle is what you're used to experiencing, a smoother route will not only make you uncomfortable, it will also signal to your subconscious mind that you're in potential danger. Obviously, from the viewpoint of your conscious mind you're in no danger, but that doesn't matter when your subconscious mind is in the driver's seat. The struggle is likely within your comfort zone. Remember, no prize is awarded for those who endure the most hardship before they reach their goal. Keep that truth in mind as you move forward, and commit to questioning your way of doing things, if, in fact, your way of doing things isn't fulfilling you.

The Benefit of Staying Stuck

Beyond the comfort that we often find in the struggle itself, remaining stuck in place has its benefits. When you're stuck, your subconscious mind knows exactly what to expect. Even your apathy or the frustration that comes with being at a standstill is predictable. Your subconscious mind loves the familiarity of knowing what's coming next, and it couldn't care less if you're happy about it or not. Staying stuck comes with an excessive amount of security, but it's just another sneaky form of self-sabotage that slowly eats away at your dreams and goals.

Contrary to popular belief, staying stuck doesn't mean you're not striving toward your goals or refusing to take action; it simply means you're not making any substantial progress in the direction you want. This is such a sneaky form of self-sabotage because you might not even realize you're doing it. After all, you are taking action and trying to move forward. Those actions are simply a distraction because the results you achieve tell a completely different story—one of staying stuck in place and going nowhere fast.

Maybe you aren't able to clearly identify where this tendency shows up in your own life just yet. However, I'm sure you've noticed self-sabotaging behaviors of this kind among your friends. I noticed this scenario playing out time and time again with my friend, Steve. Steve was a hopeless romantic, but he learned at a young age, from observing his parents' relationship, that love was hard. So, it's not surprising that as an adult, he would inadvertently sabotage and end every relationship he got into that was remotely healthy. His relationships that started off with turmoil and struggle (whether through excessive arguments, childish behaviors, or scandalous affairs) were the ones where he was certain his partner was the love of his life.

Any outside observer would have wondered what on earth he was thinking because his actions didn't match his desires in the slightest. The truth is that on some level, he couldn't completely change his choices in the love department until he reprogrammed his subconscious mind. As you know, facts, desires, and logic are no match for beliefs. Your beliefs will drive your behavior, just as Steve's beliefs did for him. Even though Steve's behavioral patterns didn't serve him, at least his subconscious mind knew what to expect. Safety and security dwell in the expected.

CHAPTER 2
REAL VS. IMAGINARY

"Infinite power resides in your imagination."

- Neville Goddard

One of the most fascinating aspects of the inner mind is its inability to differentiate between what has occurred in real life and what has been imagined. This incapacity makes a lot of sense because, as I've stated before, the subconscious isn't logical; it just takes in information as it comes and accepts it. Therefore, it's almost as if the things you visualize and imagine are processed in the same manner as your real-life experiences, which can be both a blessing and a curse. It's a blessing if you know how to harness this power to work in your favor and create the reality you want to experience in your mind first. But, if you're reckless and constantly imagine the worst-case scenarios unfold or replay scenes of perpetual struggle and defeat in your life, this gift can quickly turn into a curse. The key is to not allow your imagination to go rogue and create disastrous scenes and visuals. *Don't let your imagination go rogue!*

A prime example of this phenomenon is the depth of the emotions you feel when you wake up from a vivid dream. I've heard countless stories of women who dream their partner is cheating on them (when in reality their partner is sleeping soundly next to them), only to wake up and realize it was just a dream. Even though on a conscious level they have the evidence to comprehend that the situation wasn't real, they still feel the same emotions they would if their partner was having an affair in real life ... at least for a few minutes after they wake up. In the same way, I've heard many stories about people having a romantic dream about a platonic friend or co-worker. Days later, when they see the person they dreamed about, those lovey-dovey dream feelings suddenly come flooding back (usually briefly).

Are they secretly in love with their co-worker or best friend of ten years? Probably not. It's far more likely that their subconscious mind (remember, this is the place where all those emotions are stored) places both authentic experiences and imaginary situations into the same category and can't differentiate between the two.

You can certainly find some benefits to this aspect of the subconscious mind if you're willing to look at it from a different angle. The truth is, a slight change in perspective can easily turn what some may view as a limitation into a life-changing opportunity. You can begin to instill new beliefs within your subconscious mind by imagining new outcomes. You have the ability to transform old stories and memories and create new habits by visualizing a new scenario. Once you realize that you have the power to achieve a new end result by simply seeing it in your mind's eye first— before it manifests into your physical reality—what you can achieve is limitless.

See It Before It Manifests

A 2018 University of Colorado Boulder study shows that imagining a threat activates the same parts of the brain as experiencing it, which suggests that your imagination is a powerful tool you can use to overcome phobias and fears. In a similar fashion, you can utilize your imagination to enhance your life in a variety of ways, from improving your golf swing and achieving career goals to overcoming anxiety.

When I work with a client to create change through hypnotherapy, I use the power of visualization in each session. Often, I'll paint a mental image and they'll instinctively add their own details, making the picture in their mind's eye their own. While this method is remarkably effective for a wide range of issues, I especially love to use it with my clients who are struggling with test anxiety.

To illustrate, Jill was a client of mine who came in for help to ease her test anxiety. She was scheduled to take the LSAT in a couple of months, and to put it mildly, she was freaking out. Having never experienced any form of test anxiety in the past, she was truly thrown for a loop when she started taking her LSAT prep tests. These were just practice tests, but for whatever reason, every time she sat down to take one of them, she felt an overwhelming amount of anxiety—so much so that she would forget everything she studied. Then she went to take the LSAT for the first time. Once she sat down to take the test, she felt a sudden wave of anxiety set in. She was so jittery that she couldn't comfortably select the answers on the tablet she's been provided, and after a few minutes of trying to push through it, her mind went completely blank. It seemed like no matter how well prepared she was or how much time she had spent studying, it didn't make a difference.

I recall her holding back tears as she explained that she had been working toward becoming an attorney since she was in middle school, and now, as a woman in her mid-twenties, she wasn't sure if her dream was within reach. She didn't know if it was feasible anymore. I'll never forget when she said to me, "If I can't pass the LSAT, I don't know what I'll do. This is what I've wanted since I was a little girl."

Jill was holding onto her last bit of hope; she was eager to get to the point where she could feel calm and at ease during her second attempt at the LSAT. It's important to understand that Jill was extremely analytical by nature, and she was also very skeptical. In general, I can say the same for many attorneys, physicians, engineers, and other fact-driven professionals. This analytical bent didn't mean that she wasn't going to see results with her hypnotherapy sessions, but it did mean that she might possibly require a bit more time and effort to get into a relaxed state, as opposed to a client who was less analytically inclined.

In my experience, test anxiety can often stem from a unique combination of a lack of confidence, an overwhelming amount of pressure (whether self-induced, brought on by outsiders, or both), and an extreme amount of effort. The students' lack of confidence creates a lingering sense of self-doubt that emerges during the test. The pressure they feel can lead to freezing or feeling like they forgot everything they learned. The intense amount of effort they put forth exhausts them, while at the same time it never feels like enough.

Jill was dealing with all three of these variables. So, during each hypnotherapy session, imagining the desired outcome was key for her. First and foremost, doing so allowed her to "see" herself succeed for the very first time.

Up until our first session, she had been replaying her first failed attempt in her mind on repeat. Using her imagination to experience the feeling of taking the LSAT without lingering self-doubt and internal pressure gave her the clarity and confirmation for which she was looking. Fortunately, in Jill's case, she knew she would be taking her test in the same location as her first attempt. This was not a vital factor in her success with hypnotherapy, but it was certainly useful in the sense that she already had an idea of what her testing site would look like.

One of the key components of her hypnotherapy sessions was for her to visualize her success before she achieved it. In order to do this, she visualized herself arriving at her testing site feeling calm and collected. She saw herself walking up the steps to the test location, and feeling the chair beneath her as she sat down and prepared for the test to start. We walked through each aspect of the LSAT, from her arrival to her departure once the test was over.

She was surprised that she was able to feel calm and confident in this process. The best part is that this feeling remained even when she went to take her practice tests. The subconscious pressure and lack of confidence she had felt previously completely vanished. While it might have felt like magic to Jill, the truth was that by visualizing the process and the outcome she desired, her subconscious mind accepted it as true. Her inner mind didn't know that her visualization was something she imagined because it felt real, even though she knew it wasn't on a conscious level.

You see, in many ways, the conscious and the subconscious mind don't communicate with one another, at least not effectively. Jill knew she was using hypnotherapy, visualization, and her imagination to create the outcome she wanted by bypassing her conscious mind and tapping directly into her subconscious. Even though she was consciously aware of this fact, she was still surprised at the result, as many people are. This surprise goes back to how our subconscious mind is committed to the struggle. We often will tell ourselves things like, "It can't be that easy!" but in actuality, it can be that easy.

When You Think You Can't Visualize

A question I am often asked is, "What should I do if I can't visualize?" Before I became a hypnotherapist, I didn't know that some people are unable to picture images in their mind's eye. However, I now know it's not uncommon. I'd like to offer you a possible alternative if you happen to fall into this category. The best part about this solution is that it is just as effective as visualizing.

Before we get into the specifics, let me say that I've

found a large portion of people who believe they cannot visualize, actually can. It's not that they are incapable, but rather their notion about visualization is a bit skewed. This typically occurs because some people mistake visualization with the actual "eyes wide open" type of sight. The truth is that most of us, aside from a few outliers, don't visualize with vivid clarity; however, we're still capable of doing so to some degree.

Let me ask you this. When you're scrolling through social media and you see a group photo that a friend has posted, how do you recognize them in the picture? How do you differentiate between who you know in that image and who you haven't met? You do so by tapping into a visual reference within your mind's eye and then comparing it to the picture. Obviously, this comparison is made in the background at the subconscious level, but even so, it's happening. *Visual references*

To further demonstrate what I mean, let me give you another example of this visual reference point: if someone were to ask you to describe your office (where you likely spend most of your day), chances are you'd be able to provide a fairly accurate account of the environment. That's because you can 'see' it in some capacity. Whether your visualization is incredibly vivid and full of details or not, it doesn't take away from the fact that you can "see" your office well enough to describe it.

As a matter of fact, you can take this example and turn it into an exercise you can use to enhance your ability to visualize. Close your eyes and see yourself walking around your office. Notice the details around you. An easy way to do this is to pick a letter and look for objects that begin with that letter as you make your way around your office in your mind's eye. For instance, let's say you choose the letter "D." In your mind, you would navigate through your office while identifying all the things that start with that letter, such as the office building doors, your desk, the drawers of your desk, and so on.

In my experience, a slight shift in perspective can make a significant impact when it comes to visualizing. I've found that when someone has hangups around the concept, sometimes it's not that they can't visualize, but rather that they have an outdated idea in their head of what visualization is. Being open to embracing a new outlook and being willing to change your perspective on visualization can make all the difference.

Seeing vs. Knowing

When the concept of visualization feels like too much of a stretch, many people can identify with a very simple kind of "knowing," rather than actually "seeing."

Later on, we'll discuss a different type of "knowing" that isn't as simple. So to minimize confusion, I'm going to refer to this particular type of knowing as a "simple kind of knowing."

The best way to describe this "simple kind of knowing" to which I'm referring is through an example like the one below.

Suppose I want to do a mental exercise that requires me to imagine I'm walking in a forest, but I don't see myself walking. I also don't see the forest. I don't even hear anything. Even so, for the purpose of the exercise, I know I am walking in the forest right now.

Similar to "seeing" the outcome you desire prior to experiencing it in real life, stepping into this "simple kind of knowing" is nothing more than an active choice you make.

You don't need to do anything to experience this "simple kind of knowing." The way I see it, this knowing is very similar to imagining the outcome you desire, in that you don't need to do anything special (no five-step process you should follow) in order to imagine. Instead, you simply set the intention/make the active choice to imagine, and then you do so.

While the simplicity of this knowing can certainly make it seem like an alternative option that's almost too easy or basic to lead to anything productive, I assure you that's not the case. Making the active choice to connect with this "simple kind of knowing" has significant benefits.

In making the active choice to tap into this "simple kind of knowing," you set the groundwork for further clarity and a stronger relationship with your subconscious mind. Over time, your ability to "see" and "hear" through your mind's eye will strengthen. The images you visualize and the sounds you hear will become clearer and easier to pick up on. At some point, you may even find that details begin to emerge on their own without your conscious involvement or active engagement (which is a sign that your subconscious mind is communicating with you).

Remember, it doesn't always have to be complicated to be effective. In this case, it all comes down to making the active choice to connect with this "simple kind of knowing." *↳ visualization*

Act As If

Chances are, you've heard people say, "Fake it until you make it." This is a common approach many people use to boost their self-esteem. The general idea is that if you pretend to be confident, over time you will become more confident. Seems simple enough, right? But it's a little difficult to imagine that a concept so straightforward could be effective because as humans we underestimate our ability to manipulate our thoughts to our advantage. You must remember: you have the power to convince yourself of your success, and as a result, experience that success.

When dealing with the issue of visualization, you can use these often-underestimated skills to your advantage by "acting as if." What does that mean? Basically, you can train yourself to recognize your ability to visualize by acting as if you can, or pretending. Just like an actor takes on a role and lives within that space for the length of the film, you can take on the mindset of someone who has no problem visualizing. After a short period of time, your ability to "act as if" will likely turn into your ability to recognize that you can visualize.

Feel the Feelings

Without question, visualization can be an immensely powerful way to reprogram your subconscious beliefs and fast-track your ability to achieve goals. If you're anything like me, you might be curious how something so basic can create such a significant change. When you visualize, you get a glimpse of what is to come as you "see" your goal achieved before it plays out in real life. Naturally, this picture helps your mind begin to accept that your goal is within reach. After all, you have already witnessed it! But "seeing" yourself achieve your goal isn't the standalone reason why visualization is so effective. A big part of the transformation that is often overlooked is the emotions you feel when you're visualizing the outcome you want.

Your ability to reprogram your subconscious mind is directly tied to the emotions you feel when you visualize. The visual imagery alone is not the active component in creating change. In the same way that imagining your success allows your mind to accept new potential possibilities, feeling the emotions associated with your success solidifies your desired outcome in your subconscious mind. Therefore, being able to feel the emotions of your desired outcome is essential. In some ways, visualization is merely a means to get to those feelings.

I like to think of it like this. Suppose you are heading out on a road trip with a specific endpoint in mind, and only one highway separates you from your destination. To get to where you want to go, all you need to do is hop in a vehicle, make your way onto the highway, and drive. You can take any vehicle you want; it makes no difference whether you decide to travel in a red SUV, a white truck, or a black sports car—as long as your foot is on the gas pedal and you stay on the highway, you will reach your destination.

Similar to that highway, experiencing the feelings of your future success is the path toward your goals. Additionally, as long as you get on the highway and start driving, the vehicle you choose to travel in is inconsequential. <u>In the same way, the approach you decide to take to feel the emotions of achieving your goals doesn't matter, as long as you feel them.</u>

I share this concept to help put your mind at ease if you feel like you're unable to visualize the outcome you desire. If at this point you're simply "acting as if" to the best of your ability, that's quite alright. You can use other vehicles (approaches) to bring the future feelings you want to achieve to life. As long as you can feel the emotions associated with your desired outcome as if it was already your reality, you can experience the same beneficial outcome of visualization.

Harness Your Sense of Hearing

As you now know, visualization isn't the only way to feel the emotions of your desired outcome. One of my favorite methods to achieve an outcome similar to visualization is to rely more heavily on the sense of hearing.

When you're in a relaxed state, rather than focusing your attention entirely on the mental picture you're trying to create in your mind, try focusing on the sounds you will hear when you have achieved your desired outcome. So, if your ultimate goal is to run your best marathon, you could tap into the sound of a cheering crowd as you cross the finish line.

This method is highly effective in a variety of situations. It's fairly obvious how beneficial it can be when the goal you're trying to achieve comes with a significant amount of external praise, but what about when the goal isn't to do well in a sport? Or when the results you're striving to achieve don't result in a cheering crowd? I'll use Jill's story as an example to showcase how this technique can still be incredibly effective.

As Jill was striving to pass the LSAT, she couldn't exactly tap into a slew of raving fans who would be there cheering her on with an endless amount of praise once she left the testing site. But she could tap into her joyful response from time to time, like when she got into the car after her test and immediately called her mom to tell her the good news. Looking even further down her timeline, she could have probably heard herself sobbing tears of joy when she realized she had been accepted into the law school of her choice, which was a direct result of her remaining calm and passing the LSAT.

I believe we often take the power of sound for

granted. But if you've ever watched a horror movie without the sound on, you know that without being able to hear the creepy music and shrieks of horror in the background, even the scariest scenes can seem pretty uneventful and even dull. The absence of sound has the ability to diminish the intensity of our experience. I'd say that's pretty powerful! Not only that, but certain sounds can instantly transport us to another time and place in our mind's eye.

Have you ever randomly heard a song from a couple of decades ago that immediately brought you back to your past? If so, you've felt the emotional impact of sound. You can use the power of sound to your advantage when you're in a relaxed state by imagining and even hearing yourself engage in or overhear a conversation that will intensify your feelings about your future success.

Mantra = Sound
Hear yourself succeeding

A Sense of Knowing

One of the things I enjoy most about working in personal development is the people. Generally, I've found that the type of people who seek out-of-the-box methods and different approaches to improve their lives are often big dreamers. Their goals and ambitions push them outside of their comfort zone. Sometimes the vision they hold for their future is far beyond anything that anyone in their lives can even relate to. As a result, they often hear people say their goals are illogical and completely unattainable, but that doesn't matter to them. They don't waiver. They keep dreaming. Sure, they may pivot here or there, take a break to catch their breath from time to time, or even get sidetracked for long periods of time with other smaller goals. But their big dreams stay solid; they are always present in the back of their minds.

When our goals and dreams seem far off (meaning they are completely out of the realm of what we are accustomed to), it can be challenging to preemptively feel our future feelings of success. The main reason for the mind block is simple: you may be unfamiliar with the feelings you're chasing (at least at a conscious level). Even if you can recognize the feelings of your future success, they may seem so far out of reach that it's a challenge to step fully into and embody them in a way that gets you closer to your goal.

Fortunately, you can use another strategy to achieve results similar to embodying future feelings of success, which is to tap into your sense of inner knowing. You can bring your dreams to life by learning how to rely more heavily on your intuition and then using this sense of "knowing" as confirmation.

Before I break down each step that goes into developing this sense of inner knowing, it's important to understand what a sense of inner knowing is and what it is not. I like to think of it as an intuitive nudge that guides you to go in one direction as opposed to another. Similar to how you would use a compass as a tool to show direction, your sense of inner knowing is one way your subconscious mind provides you with direction.

When you recognize your sense of inner knowing on a conscious level, you'll quickly realize that it's a very distinct experience—once you experience it, you know. Although it's an intangible concept and difficult to define, the experience itself is unmistakable. Essentially, you either receive a strong sense of knowing that originates from an intuitive source within, or you don't. But when you do, it is so incredibly apparent that it would be a challenge for you to dismiss it, even if you wanted to. To put it simply, when you know, you know.

You might be reading this and thinking, "Well, I'm not very intuitive, so I guess I'm out of luck." If so, I want to encourage you to not give up just yet. Even if you have spent your entire life up until this point making decisions and relying solely on facts and figures, I still have good news for you: you can strengthen your intuitive nature and sense of inner knowing. In doing so, it will become apparent that you can use this inner knowing to your advantage, even if you deem yourself to be currently lacking in the intuition department.

Understanding Intuition

To strengthen your intuitive nature and inner knowing, you must gain a thorough understanding of your intuition. The most effective way to do this is to dismantle the seemingly vague concept of intuition by breaking it down into more digestible bits. Intuition is not often understood properly and is therefore misinterpreted. However, by developing a solid baseline level of understanding, you can minimize potential misinterpretations.

So, what is intuition anyway? Intuition is the ability to comprehend something immediately, without thinking about it, and without the need for conscious reasoning. In the same way, intuitive nudges are an immediate knowing (such as knowing the next step to take, knowing you're on the right path, or even having a deep sense of knowing that your situation is going to work out).

When you make a decision (whether it's in your best interest or derived from pre-existing limiting beliefs), you do so through conscious thought. So, if you catch yourself actively trying to pick between one option or another through logic or a list of facts, it's safe to say you're leaning more toward making a conscious decision and not following an intuitive nudge. The same is true if you find yourself consulting others for their opinion or talking yourself into making one choice over another through facts and figures.

Intuitive nudges, on the other hand, often defy logic and bypass your conscious reasoning. In order to use logic to justify one action over the other, you must involve your conscious mind. But intuitive nudges (the basis for a sense of inner knowing) are present without conscious thought. They are just there. No amount of logical reasoning or factual information can erase the underlying feeling (or knowing, rather) that occurs when you go against your intuition. While it's true that facts, figures, and data can reinforce why you should (at least from a logical perspective) select one choice over another (like deciding to go with option A instead of option B), it's not enough to quell your intuitive nudge.

These nudges may not necessarily be as glaringly obvious as a conscious statement that pops into your head such as, "take a left on the next street." Instead, they are more of a subconscious truth that serves as a guide; one that emerges without conscious thought. So in some ways, your conscious mind is off the hook when it comes to tapping into your sense of knowing.

Knowing that you can safely lean on your intuition during certain moments in life is truly priceless. But many people don't ever experience this sense of security. Getting a good handle on their intuition can feel as impossible as grabbing ahold of a cloud; no matter how hard they try, they can't grasp anything tangible. So naturally, many of us go through life relying solely on more concrete concepts (like facts and data) because it seems easier. Don't misunderstand me—nothing is wrong with following facts, figures, data, and consulting sources outside of yourself to make informed decisions. However, if you navigate through life without any sort of reliance on your intuition, you're selling yourself short.

Think of your intuition as a tool, and the more useful the tools in your toolbox are, the greater chance you have to succeed in all you set out to accomplish. Through a thorough understanding of intuition, you will know how to differentiate your existing intuitive nudges from other things (like underlying fears and deeply embedded habits, for instance), making the process of allowing your intuitive nudges to guide you an easy one.

As you can tell, intuition and the intuitive nudges associated with it are fairly straightforward, which makes it all the more curious that they're so often misinterpreted. You see, the lack of understanding around intuition isn't because it's an incredibly complex topic. It's a rather simple concept.

Three key factors stand in the way of developing a strong relationship with your intuition:

- Being unable to spot the difference between intuition and the past
- Having difficulty distinguishing intuition from

wishful thinking
- Not knowing when it's appropriate to trust your intuition

The reason so many people don't understand intuition and therefore are susceptible to misinterpreting it is that they don't know how to separate true intuition from their future and their past. They don't know how to differentiate what they want to happen in the future (wishful thinking) and/or their own projections from past experiences (such as lingering fears) from what their intuition is trying to tell them.

Past Projections

The line between intuition and past projections is blurry. It is odd that two seemingly vastly different concepts are so challenging to tell apart, and yet on the surface they seem to be. While they can certainly appear to blend together, when you dig a little deeper, the difference between them becomes clear.

Following your intuition provides a sense of peace and calm that feels complete in and of itself. Whereas following guidance based on past projections doesn't feel satisfying because guidance based on our past projections is typically trying to mitigate lingering underlying fear, and it shows. It reveals itself through the way your body feels when you go down that path. You get a sense of uneasiness and uncertainty that resolves itself once you lean into intuition.

The next time you need to differentiate between intuition and past projections, notice what happens in your body when you pick one option over the other. Does your body feel both relaxed and exhilarated simultaneously? Or does your body feel uneasy and do you question your reality? Your body will provide you with the clarity you seek; all you have to do is listen.

Here are some other questions you can ask yourself and sit with to determine whether you're leaning into intuition or fear based on past projections:

- What effect does saying "yes" to this idea have on me? Does it feel expansive or restrictive?
- Is this experience reminiscent of a feeling from my past?
- What's going on underneath the surface?

[Handwritten margin note: Listen to your body]

Wishful Thinking

On the other side of the spectrum is a similar issue when it comes to separating intuition from wishful thinking. Once again, the primary difference between wishful thinking and intuition is how you feel while receiving the information. Intuition is persistent. It's felt in the body in a very settled and solid manner. Conversely, wishful thinking often shows up in the body as tension and restlessness.

Here's a simple exercise you can use to check in with your body to confirm whether you're following your intuition or something else.

1. Place your hand on your heart and take a couple of deep, relaxing breaths.
2. Say a statement that you know to be true out loud. This could be anything from your phone number to the city you were born in.
3. As you say your statement, take note of how your body responds.
4. Next, take your hand off your heart and relax for a moment. When you're ready, place your hand on your heart once again.
5. This time, say a statement that is not true.
6. As you say this false statement, bring your awareness inward to your body and notice its response.

Chances are that when you say your false statement, you will feel vastly different within your body than when you say your true statement. You can use your physical body as a means to gauge what is true and what is false. In the same way, you can repeat this process, swapping out one possible option for another and noticing which one makes you feel physically calm, content, and at peace. That's likely the path toward which your intuition is guiding you.

In situations where you go against an intuitive nudge, the best outcome you can hope for is that the facts and data you've relied on will take you from, "I'm not sure about this" to "Okay, that makes sense, but it still doesn't feel right." Again, as you and I are both aware, something making sense and something feeling right can be two very different things. What it comes down to is this: when you follow your intuitive nudges, it feels right even if it doesn't make sense.

Trust Your Intuition... Sometimes

Knowing how to tune into what your body is trying to tell you is key when it comes to accurately identifying your intuition. Even so, you still may be hesitant to follow your intuition all the time, even when your body tells you it's the right move.

I believe logic and intuition should be relied upon equally as you navigate through life. One isn't more reliable or helpful than the other, and each has its time and place. While your intuition may not get it right 100% of the time, logic offers no guarantees either. Use your discretion and trust yourself enough to know which of the two options your specific life situations require.

With that being said, it is possible that depending upon the culture you were raised in, you were taught to place more trust in logic than in your intuition. If that's the case, you likely feel far more comfortable relying on logic to make important decisions, as it's what you've been taught to do and likely have been doing for as long as you can remember. But armed with this self-awareness, you can use logic to your benefit as you branch out and learn to trust your intuitive side. This buildup of confidence can be accomplished by using facts and more "logical" information to reinforce your intuition.

The subconscious (intuition's source) can process more information than the logical mind, which means it bases its stance on far more information than you are consciously aware of. Therefore, incorporating intuition into your decision-making allows you to consider many aspects of your past experiences that you may have overlooked on a conscious level. Overall, the key takeaway is to recognize that your intuition is an incredibly useful tool that you may have glossed over or dismissed in the past. If so, I encourage you to explore your intuitive side a bit more, become comfortable with it, and learn not to be afraid to lean on it, especially when logic misses the mark.

Future Decision Making

The final step to strengthening your intuition (and developing your sense of inner knowing as a result) is to present more opportunities for your intuitive nudges to guide you. In general, the more chances you give yourself to lean on your intuition, the more likely you are to rely more heavily on it, and the more you rely on it, the more you will learn to trust it.

It may sound complicated, but I assure you it's not. You've already done the hardest part, which is learning to spot the difference between intuition and other factors. The secret to solidifying your relationship with your intuitive nudges isn't to manufacture unnatural opportunities. It's to simply continue to recognize the nudges as they emerge.

The best way I've found to do this is to keep yourself accountable by reflecting daily on the moments, subtle or otherwise, that you received an intuitive nudge. As you do this, any lingering fear or doubt around your intuitive nudges will begin to subside. In the same way the mysterious aspect of a new person fades once you get to know them, the unknown aspect of your intuitive nudges will subside once you develop a relationship with them. Not only that, but as you become more comfortable with your intuitive nudges, it will be easier for you to refer back to them and confirm their validity.

Keep in mind, this isn't a quick fix or an overnight solution. It's a process that requires dedication and a willingness to question and step beyond your comfort zone. You can also take some additional actions that will help speed up the process and keep you moving forward each day.

- Throughout the day, check in with yourself. Notice when you feel a sense of peace and ease. Acknowledge these moments, as they often occur after you follow an intuitive nudge.
- Talk your conscious mind out of its fear by reminding yourself what intuitive nudges truly are: a way for your subconscious mind to speak directly to your conscious mind and provide it with direction.
- Whenever you're unsure whether to follow an intuitive nudge or go the other way, stop and listen. The best way to do this is to sit down, be silent, and focus your eyes on one particular object in front of you. As you keep your focus, you will find that all of your worries and hesitations dissolve

because they aren't with you in the present moment (they are all a past thought or future projection). This exercise will allow you to listen to what your intuition is trying to tell you.

CHAPTER 3
BRING ABOUT POSITIVE CHANGE

"Imagination is everything. It is the preview of life's coming attractions."

- Albert Einstein

Everyone loves a good 'aha' moment when everything seemingly falls into place. I'm referring to those instances in life when it all clicks. Some people call them lightbulb moments. In these instances, all you've been through leading up to that point subtly fades into the background, and the answers you've been seeking for some time are revealed.

To me, the feelings experienced in these moments compare to finding the last missing puzzle piece under the couch and finally getting to complete the puzzle. It's a feeling of excitement, ease, and completion all wrapped into one experience. While it may seem, especially at the moment, like you were stuck at point A for so long and then everything changed for the better in a split second, we all know that's not entirely true. In reality, you put forth energy, time, and effort that led up to that moment of clarity.

So what is it about these 'aha' moments that feels so great? I think it's the undeniable clarity and contentment we feel. It's the polar opposite of struggle—it's total and complete alignment. Unfortunately, these lightbulb moments are rare occurrences for many people because, as discussed at length in chapter one, most people unknowingly hang on to the subconscious notion that the struggle is a prerequisite to achievement. Only when we realize we can achieve our goals without the constant struggle we're used to can we cultivate more lightbulb moments in our lives.

By subconsciously releasing even a portion of our self-imposed struggle, we let go of resistance. By letting go of resistance, we create room to allow new ideas, concepts, and insight to emerge, and we can experience a sense of all-encompassing alignment.

Time and time again, I hear from clients who tell me they're suddenly noticing an influx of 'aha' moments in their lives. They experience a series of clear and consistent insights that guide them toward their right next step. After years (sometimes decades) of waiting for clarity, the answers seemingly fall into their laps, and they can finally forge ahead toward their dreams.

You're probably wondering what the common denominator is in each of their experiences. What is the catalyst that provides them with such clarity and insight? The answer is really simplistic but highly transformative. My clients merely become aware of something you already learned in chapter one: the struggle isn't required. As they begin to question their struggle rather than take it at face value, they loosen the grip it has on them. You see, one large aspect of the struggle we often face is that it serves as a form of resistance to our goals. Questioning the struggle rather than just accepting it releases some of that resistance. In relinquishing this battle, my clients are able to finally experience the 'aha' moment that allows them to move forward toward the outcome they want.

Examples of some of these questions include:

- What would you do if the struggle wasn't required?
- How would this situation change if your success was inevitable?
- Does breaking this habit have to be hard, or could it be easier? What would that look like? How would that feel?

One client's experience in particular stands out in my mind whenever I think about incredible 'aha' moments. William was in his mid-30s and would describe himself as successful in all aspects of his life except his career. Although he felt this way, by pretty much everyone else's standards, he was doing quite well career-wise. However, it really didn't matter that anyone else considered him a success because he didn't feel that way himself.

He was a chef in Los Angeles and had been working in the restaurant industry for about 15 years when he came in to see me. He explained to me that he took a "less than traditional" approach to developing his career. He said that while the majority of chefs start out in their early 20s, grinding in hot kitchens as line cooks and working 12-hour days for years on end, only to get promoted if they're in the right place at the right time (meaning if someone else ends up suddenly leaving their current position), he took a different path. He started working in kitchens at the age of fifteen. After high school, he went to culinary school for four years, working in restaurants part-time and often as an intern. Upon graduation, he continued to work long days but moved up the ladder quickly because of his education, talent, and experience.

In comparison with others in similar positions, his career progressed quickly, but he was still unsatisfied. His lifelong dream was to open his own restaurant, but he felt stuck waiting for "the right time." Of course, "the right time" had yet to reveal itself and he wondered if it ever would. Keep in mind, William was a highly intelligent man, and he intentionally took a career path that in many ways ensured he struggled much less than his counterparts. As a result of his strategic career planning, he excelled in his career. Even so, he still wasn't where he wanted to be career-wise and was having a difficult time giving himself recognition for what he had accomplished in his life up until this point.

After his first hypnotherapy session, he was already feeling significantly better. He was able to acknowledge his success and feel proud of himself, which is something he had not felt in years. While he wasn't completely unstuck just yet, he said he felt like he had some wiggle room now. Basically, he was finally starting to feel like the path forward was becoming more tangible. He went from being able to see his future to really feeling like his future goals were within reach. His future, of course, included him opening his own restaurant without waiting any longer for the 'perfect moment' that may not ever arrive.

Upon further probing, William had a distinct 'aha' moment right before my eyes, and I have to tell you it was incredible to witness as an outside observer. Although he had taken a particular career path that resulted in his accelerated success up until this point, a part of him felt unworthy. He also felt an intense sense of guilt because he knew most of his peers weren't achieving the same level of success. He compared it to riding a bullet train while everyone else was on a bicycle.

He felt as if he was sitting comfortably, enjoying the air conditioning on the train and bypassing the hardship and struggle, while his peers were exerting intense energy on their bicycles but barely making any progress. Nevertheless, he still wanted more.

He was going through the same emotions as someone who cheated to get ahead—William had a guilty conscience. But he didn't sabotage, cheat, or deceive anyone. He simply felt guilty for his own success—the same success he'd earned and deserved. So, because he wasn't struggling alongside his peers, he was subconsciously manifesting his own struggle through feeling stuck and unable to open his own restaurant. Through hypnotherapy and prompting, he finally realized that the struggle wasn't required, and that realization changed everything. By our next session, he was not only no longer stuck and stagnant, but he had found an investor for his restaurant and was proactively taking steps to move forward with his dream.

Flash forward to today. William opened the doors to his restaurant about a month ago, and he couldn't be happier. He is finally thriving in all areas of his life, not according to everyone else, but according to him. For the first time ever, he has given himself permission to enjoy the benefits of his talents and efforts. Just as important, he is no longer subconsciously punishing himself for his well-deserved success, but is embracing it instead.

Strengthen Awareness

Perhaps you had an experience similar to William's after learning that (at least some of) your struggle is likely self-imposed and not an essential component to your progress forward. If not, that's completely alright because you will soon discover that you too can live a more joyful and fulfilling life by bypassing unnecessary difficulties. William's story illustrates that it's not so much a question of whether you're capable of experiencing more 'aha' moments in life, but rather how to tap into your inherent ability to do so.

If you've ever had to wait in line for an excessive amount of time, you probably know what it's like to feel like your patience is being tested. No one likes to wait, but that's exactly what many people find themselves doing—waiting for the next lightbulb moment when they can go from stuck to unstuck. While the clarity that moment provides is undeniably valuable, waiting for that moment doesn't get you closer to experiencing it. Even though you desperately want to feel the sense of alignment you believe that moment will provide to you, the mounting pressure you feel from waiting for it is in direct conflict with what you are trying to achieve.

Sometimes it seems like lightbulb moments are hard to come by, and waiting for them to show up is the only option. But for many people, waiting often leads to more tension and stress because they go long periods without gaining any significant insight or clear direction to move forward. On top of that pressure, they end up having to deal with the weight of feeling stuck, while being unsure of how to proceed. Sure, they could forge ahead and wing it while hoping things work out in their favor, but they will have to do so without an ounce of confidence in the direction they choose to take.

This option doesn't seem very promising, does it? Fortunately, you have another alternative: figuring out how to have more 'aha' moments. This way, you can keep the wheels in motion and continue pushing forward without a long hiatus in between, and do so without an overwhelming amount of self-doubt or fear. While you can't avoid every hurdle and challenge that life throws your way, it is possible to avoid self-inflicted struggle. The more you gain insight into the subconscious mind and understand the patterns associated with it, the stronger that awareness will become, and the stronger that awareness becomes, the more frequent 'aha' moments you will have. Being able to use this awareness to bypass some hardship is not only empowering; it's gratifying as well.

Some of my all-time favorite methods to direct the subconscious mind and strengthen this awareness include:

- Hypnotherapy
- Self-hypnosis

- Affirmations
- Probing questions specifically for the subconscious

Hypnotherapy

Over the years, hypnotherapy has and will probably continue to become more of a mainstream method for changing one's habits and behaviors. Even so, the slightest mention of the word "hypnotherapy" always prompts a handful of skeptics and a few critical reactions. More often than not, their skepticism and criticism are misguided and not due to hypnotherapy itself, but instead result from the misconceptions and lack of knowledge many people have around the topic. The reasons for these misconceptions are obvious.

The media and performative hypnotists have created a very one-sided narrative around the entire concept of hypnosis and hypnotherapy. When people hear the words "hypnotherapy" or "hypnosis," they often instantly picture a stage hypnotist, along with all the wild theatrical aspects stage hypnosis entails. However, it's a mistake to think that stage hypnosis and hypnotherapy are the same because they are not.

The false assumption that the two fields are the same has left many people with an unsettling feeling around the whole idea of hypnotherapy. But why? What is it about stage hypnosis that makes people hesitant to experience the power of their subconscious mind?

I believe this reaction is mainly due to the lack of control the subject seems to have while being in a hypnotic state. When seemingly emotionally intelligent, stable individuals go from sitting calmly in an audience to quacking like ducks on a stage with thousands of onlookers laughing at them, it's reasonable to conclude that the subject has no control over their actions or thoughts. It's not that much of a stretch to assume the person under hypnosis is merely a puppet of sorts and the hypnotist is running the show.

The truth is that the "hypnotic state" the subject is in during stage hypnosis is nothing more than the combination of a relaxed state, the subconscious mind being at the forefront, and the subject being open to accepting the hypnotist's suggestions. Suffice to say, the person experiencing hypnosis has just as much, if not more, control than the hypnotist.

Contrary to how it may appear on the surface, nobody on that stage lacks control. If the subject begins to quack like a duck or make noises like a chicken, it's because they're open to it at some level. In these cases, the reason they accept suggestions (as absurd as some of them may seem) is because they want to. The same rule applies when a person experiences hypnotherapy, with one major caveat: the suggestions are aligned with a therapeutic goal.

Although it's fairly common to lump "hypnotherapy" and "stage hypnosis" into the same category in one's mind, you should be aware of key aspects that differentiate them from one another. Stage hypnosis is hypnosis performed in front of an audience for entertainment purposes. The audience is usually involved in some capacity and the performance is often both dramatic and amusing. Conversely, hypnotherapy is essentially a relaxed state of mind with a specific therapeutic focus. The setting is typically in a hypnotherapist's office (or the client's home for remote sessions), and the experience is similar to meditation.

So while the term "hypnosis" is often used interchangeably for both stage hypnosis and hypnotherapy, they're not exactly the same thing. The key component they both have in common is that they use a relaxed state (sometimes called a trance-like state) to bring the subconscious mind to the forefront in order to achieve some sort of goal. Stage hypnosis has the goal of entertaining, while hypnotherapy (also referred to as therapeutic hypnosis) has a therapeutic focus.

Even with all the knowledge in the world about hypnotherapy, you may still have some reservations. I've had many clients walk through my office door equipped with a willingness to change, but also carrying a lingering hesitation around the unknown. In these situations, I've found the best way to alleviate their anxiety or apprehension around the subject of hypnotherapy is to reiterate two truths:

1. Although hypnotherapy is an altered state, it isn't magic. It can't make you forget where or who you are. In the same respect, it can't make you do things you don't want to do or accept suggestions you aren't willing to accept. In other words, your free will doesn't leave your side during a hypnotherapy session.

2. You've already experienced the "trance-like" state of hypnotherapy/ therapeutic hypnosis before… even if you've never stepped foot into a hypnotherapist's office.

A common question I'm often asked about hypnotherapy is, "What is it going to feel like?" The answer to this question falls in line with the second truth, as stated above: you've been in a hypnotic state before, and you probably didn't even recognize it. The feelings associated with being in a hypnotic state are commonly described as extreme relaxation and openness, both mentally and emotionally. Many people also say that time seems to go by faster. For instance, when emerging from an hour-long session, clients will sometimes say the session felt like it was only 10-15 minutes long, although the clock clearly displays otherwise.

Perhaps you've heard of "highway hypnosis." Highway hypnosis is the phenomenon that happens when you drive long distances with no recollection of having consciously done so. People who drive long distances for work, such as truck drivers, frequently experience this occurrence. Maybe you've even experienced it for yourself, but if not, don't worry. You likely have experienced an even more common example of this phenomenon.

It goes something like this. You've had a long day of work, and you're ready to head home, get into some comfy loungewear, kick up your feet, and relax. You get in your car and start to head home, taking the same route you usually take. Before you know it, you're pulling up to your driveway. As you put your car in park, you sit there in silence for a moment, wondering where the last 15 minutes of your drive went. You don't remember driving the second half of your drive home at all. You have no recollection of stopping at any of the usual stoplights, merging onto the highway, getting off on your exit ... none of that. It's all a complete blur.

The state you were in during your drive home is the feeling of hypnosis. That is the trance-like state some people are so hesitant to experience. Many find comfort in the realization that they have already experienced hypnosis (even just on occasion during their daily commute), and hopefully you will, too.

Self-Hypnosis

Another complement to hypnotherapy, and something I encourage all of my clients to do in addition to their hypnotherapy sessions, is called self-hypnosis. A simple way to understand self-hypnosis is to think of it as a hypnotherapy session facilitated by you (where you will act as both the hypnotherapist and the client). During self-hypnosis, you enter a trance-like state at will and then use imagery and the power of suggestion to overcome problems and improve your life and overall wellbeing. You do this exercise entirely on your own, without the help of any outsiders or other influences. This is an especially helpful approach for those who cannot break free from their misconceptions about losing control while in hypnosis. It's a great way for them to experience hypnosis while guiding themselves through it.

The process of self-hypnosis is similar to meditation. One of the key differences between the two is that during meditation, the goal is to clear your mind. During self-hypnosis, you want to focus on the outcome you desire (or whatever it is you're striving to achieve).

Let's say you want to use self-hypnosis to increase your confidence. You can use the step-by-step self-hypnosis process below to achieve your goal to boost your self-esteem.

1. Get into a comfortable position by sitting up straight with your feet planted on the floor and your hands resting comfortably on your lap.

2. Focus your attention on something above eye level, such as a spot on the wall in front of you. Take a couple of deep, relaxing breaths and slowly close your eyes.

3. Next, focus your attention on your body, starting at the top of your head. Move your attention down your body, and as you do this, repeat a calming phrase or keyword to yourself, like "relax."

4. Allow your deep focus and the soothing sense of relaxation to flow from the top of your head all the way down through your body to the bottom of your feet.

5. Count backward from five to zero, with the intention that with every descending number you will go deeper into that relaxed state, and at zero you'll reach complete relaxation. Focus on your breathing and use it as an anchor that guides you to feel progressively calmer.

6. As you did in step four, allow the deep focus and sense of calmness to flow from the top of your head all the way down through your body

to the bottom of your feet.

7. Next, visualize yourself standing at the top of a staircase. See yourself walking down the staircase, counting down from 20 as you go. Notice how much more relaxed you get with each step you take and every descending number you say.

8. When you reach zero, tell yourself "deep sleep."

9. Repeat confidence-boosting suggestions to yourself.

10. When you're ready, count up from zero to five and open your eyes.

It might seem like a lot to remember, but it's fairly straightforward once you do it once or twice. The one step I've noticed people occasionally have trouble with is step nine: repeating suggestions to yourself. This is perhaps the most important step of all, so getting it right is vital. The main issue is that most people don't know what suggestions to say to themselves.

A quick way to come up with impactful suggestions to use during self-hypnosis is to change your perspective, which you can do by asking yourself, "What words of encouragement would I tell someone else who was trying to achieve a simple goal?"

When the goal is to boost your self-esteem, for example, your answers might be similar to the following:

- "Every day, I get closer to bringing my dreams to life. I'm proud of myself!"
- "I'm vibrant, confident, and proud of who I am."
- "I've accomplished so much and will continue to do so."
- "I love who I am and who I'm becoming."

I have two rules of thumb you should stick to when forming positive suggestions to tell yourself while in self-hypnosis. The first is to keep your focus on one specific goal at a time. The second is to make sure you positively phrase your suggestions. You'll discover why this positivity is so important as you learn about the next method to strengthen your awareness.

Affirmations

You can't get around the fact that what you say to yourself matters. The importance of positive self-talk might not be groundbreaking news to you, but that doesn't take away its significance. The subconscious mind is incapable of accepting two conflicting ideas or concepts simultaneously. Therefore, it's nearly impossible to speak negatively to yourself and at the same time feel good about yourself. So, it only makes sense to actively commit to speaking to yourself in a way that supports your growth and overall wellbeing.

If you still aren't sold on the idea that negatively talking to yourself affects your wellbeing, a shift in perspective may convince you otherwise. A good principle to follow is 'if you wouldn't say it to your best friend, don't say it to yourself.' Even if you generally take even the harshest criticism extraordinarily well, I think it's safe to surmise that you would rather be on the receiving end of positive self-talk as opposed to negative self-talk.

If you've previously practiced any form of positive self-talk, it has likely been in the context of an inner dialogue between you and yourself, almost like a one-sided conversation. Among the various forms of positive self-talk, affirmations are extremely popular due to both their simplicity and their effectiveness.

Affirmations are essentially positive statements that you tell yourself repeatedly. This form of positive self-talk, paired with repetition, eventually works its way to your subconscious mind. Since the subconscious mind cannot accept two opposing ideas simultaneously, it accepts what is repeatedly reinforced, which is why it's so important that you are not only aware of what you say to yourself, but are proactively choosing the right form of self-talk. Choose positive self-talk that gets you closer to your goals and helps you accomplish your dreams.

Affirmations are one of the simplest ways to reinforce your desires at a subconscious level. Keep two guidelines in mind when creating affirmations:

1. Don't use filler words like, "no," "not," "can't," "never," and so on, because your subconscious mind will hone in on the main points of your stated affirmation while bypassing filler words entirely. Instead, focus on the outcome you desire.

2. Avoid using negative keywords such as "anxiety," "worried," and "afraid," as they reiterate what you don't want. Stick to the positive.

Keeping these guidelines in mind, the affirmation, "I never skip my workout" would not be useful if I were trying to accomplish the goal of exercising more consistently. I would literally be reinforcing exactly what I don't want: skipping my workout. Instead, a much more effective affirmation would be, "I always show up for my workout."

Below are a couple of examples of affirmations that have been revised to avoid any potential subconscious misinterpretation and increase the likelihood of you getting the outcome you desire.

- "I no longer crave sweets and sugary foods." → "I crave healthy foods and fill up on fresh

vegetables and fruit."
- "My anxiety is fading away and I'm less worried than I used to be." → "I feel calm and collected at all times and in all situations."

As you can see from the above examples, a nearly foolproof way to ensure that your affirmations are in your best interest is to flip them around to the positive and keep the focus on either the present or future, rather than the past. It's not about what you want to avoid or what habit you want to eliminate, but rather the future outcome or the habits that will result from that outcome.

The most common reason people avoid affirmations is that they know (on a conscious level) that they're not where they want to be yet. So, if you find yourself repeating affirmations and thinking, "But ... this isn't true," you're not alone.

You can combat this internal struggle in two ways. The first option is to add the phrase "in the process of" to your affirmation. Using the affirmation "I feel calm and collected at all times and in all situations" as an example, you would simply restate the affirmation, telling yourself something along the lines of, "I am in the process of feeling calm and collected at all times and in all situations."

I find this addition to be an especially useful and

easy way to ease the part of your conscious mind that brings doubt to the surface. What I love most about this method is that it's simple, and it works for nearly every affirmation you could think to recite. It serves as a way to ease into a new idea or concept without feeling as if you're trying to convince or trick yourself into believing something that you have yet to achieve. Plus, it's a nice reminder that you don't have to reach a finish line when it comes to affirming your desires and that it's more than okay to be in the process of achieving or manifesting your goals.

Questions for the Subconscious

You can combat the internal dialogue that questions whether your affirmations are true at that moment in another way. I like to call it "questions for the subconscious." While affirmations are statements used to affirm your desires and goals, questions for the subconscious are questions formed around the assumption that your desires have already been achieved.

These questions are both empowering and thought-provoking. They are structured in a specific manner that affirms the outcome you want (similar to affirmations), but instead of convincing your subconscious mind through repetition, they give your subconscious mind a chance to gather information and convince itself. In other words, unlike typical questions that require a response and often lead to a back-and-forth dialogue, these questions are specifically directed toward your subconscious mind, which means you don't have to consciously seek out the answers. Instead, your subconscious mind will seek out the answer for you.

I'm often asked, "How can I trust that my subconscious mind will come up with the right answers?" That's a great question and a valid concern because if you're asking these questions then your current beliefs likely conflict with your goal. But this form of subconscious questioning works well and is reasonably safe to rely on for good reason.

As discussed in the previous chapters, your subconscious mind is constantly looking for evidence to reconfirm and strengthen your current beliefs. However, that doesn't mean you won't have experiences that provide evidence to the contrary. It's just where your subconscious mind is placing the majority of its focus. Therefore, when you structure your question in a way that puts your focus on the new outcome that you desire, your subconscious mind will gather information that proves it to be true.

I'll give you an example. Let's say that for whatever reason you hold the belief that most of the cars on the road today are red. Now, a quick search online would reveal that statistically, your belief is untrue; most cars on the road are white or black. However, let's say you don't care. You're set in your ways for whatever reason, and you're not consciously trying to change your belief (however inaccurate it may be). As a result, your subconscious mind stands firm, pushing the validity (or lack thereof) of your current belief aside. Therefore, when you're out and about, your subconscious mind will continue to provide you with evidence that your belief is true, regardless of the facts. In other words, you'll notice all the red cars.

Now, of course, different-colored vehicles are all around you, but those fade into the background, as your subconscious mind has no use for them at that moment. So, you may find yourself stopped at a red light surrounded by white cars, but your focus will remain on the one red car next to you.

However, be aware that the subconscious mind does remember what you deem significant. Therefore, while you might not be consciously focused on all the other cars driving down the road alongside you, your inner mind is still taking note (at least to some extent). But let's suppose you want to challenge your current belief. Maybe you fact-checked yourself and learned that statistically far more white cars are on the road than red cars. You then present a question to your subconscious mind that aligns with the new belief or outcome you want such as, "Why are so many white cars on the road lately?"

Since your subconscious mind retains your significant past experiences, it can search through them to deliver you memories and information that are in alignment with the new belief you want to instill: in this case, that more white cars are on the road than any other color.

When a question is asked in a way that implies you have already achieved your goal, the assumption is also made that your current beliefs align with your goal. The question is so incredibly direct that your subconscious mind has no space to go in another direction, which allows it to seek out and find reasons why your desired outcome must be true.

The key to ensuring these subconscious questions are effective is found in the way the questions are formed. Keep a couple of things in mind when formulating your question for your subconscious mind:

- Assume the outcome you desire has been achieved. If this assumption feels like too far of a stretch, then break down your goal into more feasible steps.
- Change your perspective from "I'm looking for answers," to "I'm collecting evidence to prove my point."

Let's say that the outcome you desire is to make more friends. Maybe you feel like you don't have any friends at the moment, so to assume that you're thriving in that area doesn't sit right with you. If that's the case, you can break your goal down to something a bit more digestible, like becoming more social, getting out more, or calling one friend a week to catch up. Keeping the two tips above in mind, here are a few examples of questions for your subconscious mind:

- Why is socializing second nature to me?
- Why is it so easy for me to talk to new people?
- Why does everyone want to be my friend?
- Why am I so good at making friends?

As you can see, these questions aren't complicated. They're straightforward and open the door to a variety of answers. I like to think of them as marching orders for your inner mind.

The best part about using this method of questioning is that you can simply repeat the question to yourself a couple of times per day and allow your subconscious mind to work behind the scenes and come up with the answers for you.

At some point, you will gain conscious awareness of the answers your subconscious mind has generated. This consciousness might happen sporadically in bits and pieces, or you may experience a wave of answers all at once. Once you receive these answers, you can formulate your affirmations around them to reinforce the outcome you're striving to achieve.

CHAPTER 4
YOUR STORY

"What lies behind us and what lies before us are tiny matters compared to what lies within us. And when we bring what is within us out into the world, miracles happen."

- Ralph Waldo Emerson

Without a doubt, life is full of obstacles. Regardless of who you are or where you're from, at some point life is going to present you with hurdles you'll be forced to either overcome or succumb to. No one is exempt from this universal truth. But far too many of us never ask ourselves this incredibly important question: How many of the obstacles that we face in life have we unintentionally created for ourselves?

When it comes to the mental obstacles in our lives, we often turn our experiences into stories. The problem with doing so is that these stories don't always serve us. In fact, these stories can potentially prevent us from experiencing the life we truly want. It's a sneaky but powerful form of self-sabotage, and it all comes down to the story we tell ourselves about who we are and what we're capable of achieving.

These generalized limiting beliefs serve as an overarching theme that often dictates the outcome of our lives. In situations when these stories are based on our own perceived limitations and shortcomings, giving meaning to these events isn't always beneficial or even necessary. So, if life is not going according to plan, it may be time to opt for a new narrative—one that is in alignment with the future you want.

When I refer to "the story" you tell yourself about yourself, I want to be very clear. I'm talking about the generalizations you make (whether it be aloud or to yourself) about who you are and the type of life you can lead. This narrative goes beyond a specific limiting belief such as, "I don't like to work out." A limiting story is more encompassing, with a generalized outcome such as, "Whenever I start a new workout routine, I always end up quitting. I just can't stick with it no matter how hard I try."

The difference between the two statements is significant. A specific limiting belief can certainly hold you back from the things you want to accomplish, but a limiting story is much more conclusive in that it doesn't only impact one specific facet of your life (like your physical health, for example). It often results in you giving up before you even start.

Limiting stories are the common roadblocks that keep many people stuck in a pattern of struggle, even when they know better and are fully equipped with the tools to do better. To bring about the positive change you want, you first have to change the story you tell yourself about your life, your potential, and what you are capable of accomplishing. Achieving this change is easier said than done. However, it's not an impossible task that only a select few can manage. It's well within reach for you as well, as long as you're willing to put in the work to do so. While we've already discussed the different methods that you can use to align your subconscious beliefs with your conscious desires, I want to encourage you to dive deeper and rewrite your story as one that supports your highest vision for yourself.

It's so easy to fall into the trap of allowing what we have been through to define our future, but it doesn't have to be that way. A great sense of freedom comes from letting go of your story. Now, don't get me wrong—it's essential to your growth that you look at the past patterns in your life, take ownership of your mistakes, and actively choose to learn and grow from them. However, those actions are vastly different from living in the past through an outdated and misaligned story.

When we live in the past or use our past perceived

failures to tell the story of our lives, we become our story. Our story becomes the shackles that bind us and keep us from moving toward the future we ultimately want. If you have a limiting story about your life (which most of us do), then it likely means you have been through enough to feel, at least in some way, that your future is mapped out for you based on your experiences. While that belief can certainly be true if you allow it to be, it doesn't have to be.

While the story you're living in may not be glaringly obvious to you, you have likely observed other people living within a storyline that clearly is not serving them (at least from your observation). If this dynamic rings true for you, then you're well aware that it is often a lot easier to see patterns when you observe them from an outside perspective. This tendency is very common, and the upside to it is that if you can recognize patterns within others, you can certainly learn to recognize them within yourself.

The Patterns in Other People's Lives

The other day I was talking to my dear friend, Beth, and she eagerly told me about her own experience with this dynamic. During our conversation, she recounted a series of events that occurred between her and her friend, Fay, and the patterns surrounding them. As I recall, Beth told me that everything came to a head on a dreary Friday night; the kind of night that's perfect for ordering cheap takeout and hanging out at home. She was just getting comfy on her couch and was about to start watching a new rom-com when her phone buzzed. A split second before she grabbed her phone, she had a visceral reaction. She felt herself intuitively clench her teeth at the mere thought that her friend, Fay, might be the person on the other end of the phone.

Beth's reaction wasn't because Fay was prone to inciting tension wherever she went or anything similar to that. However, Beth found herself in what could only be described as a never-ending loop with Fay, and Beth was sick and tired of it. What started as a "one-time thing" six months earlier had quickly spiraled into a cycle that kept recurring every three or four weeks. Fay would call or text Beth and confide in her that her boyfriend had broken up with her. She'd ask Beth to come over, and they'd spend the night making plans to help Fay get back on her feet. Beth would console Fay for hours, often staying up with her all night, despite feeling drained and exhausted.

Days later, Beth would find out that Fay was back together with her boyfriend. But their reconciliation was never long-lasting. Like clockwork, about three to four weeks later, Beth would hear from Fay, who would again share the news of her most recent breakup (with the same boyfriend). The cycle would continue and the two women would go round and round.

Apparently, Beth's body intuitively knew that the time had come for Fay to contact her because along with her tightly clenched teeth, Beth also noticed tension in her stomach. Sure enough, when Beth finally unlocked her phone to see who was trying to reach her, her eyes confirmed what the rest of her body already sensed: it was Fay.

Consoling Fay for what seemed like the hundredth time was the last thing Beth wanted to do. A feeling of dread consumed her at the mere thought of doing so. She asked herself, "Why would I leave my cozy condo to spend another Friday night helping a woman who clearly needs to move on from this guy?" While Beth didn't technically owe anyone an explanation for deciding to put herself and her own needs first, she still felt the desire to justify her actions to herself. So, she answered her own question aloud, "You wouldn't."

What Beth did next might surprise you as much as it did me. She completely disappeared on Fay. She never responded to her text, didn't circle back, and instead went completely silent on her. She vanished from Fay's life completely.

Now, I know you don't know Beth (so you'll have

to take my word for it), but her kindness and empathy are unmatched, which is why I was very surprised to learn that she handled this unfortunate situation with Fay in such an extreme manner. As Beth continued to recall this situation between her and Fay, one thing became very obvious to me. Beth was well aware that her approach to stopping this cycle with Fay wasn't in line with what one would expect a mature adult to do in this situation. But in the heat of the moment, Beth was really good at justifying her actions (as so many of us are) and convincing herself that she took the moral high road. She felt like the pattern showing up in Fay's life was obvious, and the solution was so simple that Fay must be purposely creating a dramatic dynamic for attention.

As the days of silence continued, Fay made countless attempts to reach out to Beth. Beth stayed silent and continued to tell herself that she would only talk to Fay once she opened her eyes and ended things with her immature boyfriend once and for all.

Now, at this point in Beth's story, I felt compassion for both women. Like so many of us, Beth was great at observing other people's lives and making judgments about what she felt was the obvious solution (from her perspective as an outsider). The problem (and the reason I picked this particular story to share with you) was that she was terrible at looking at the patterns in her own life and the story that she herself was continually stuck in.

Was it possible that Beth could be right about Fay? Absolutely! Fay might have been stuck in a story of her own creation—one that told her she couldn't make it on her own or that her worth was determined by how much she tolerated in relationships, regardless of how destructive they were. She may have grown up in a home with little structure and observed unhealthy dynamics perpetually being justified as "love." If that was the case, then Fay was living out her own self-fulfilling prophecy, whether she was aware of it or not. But whether Beth was correct in her judgments surrounding Fay was frankly irrelevant. What's truly noteworthy is that Beth was doing the exact thing she surmised Fay was doing: unconsciously playing a role in her personal story. Beth was so busy focusing on the patterns in Fay's life and judging her for staying stuck in a loop of struggle and hurt that she was unable to recognize the patterns showing up in her own life at the time.

Like Beth, many of us have experienced one-sided relationships. In these friendship dynamics, one person typically plays numerous roles, like the cheerleader, the secret-keeper, the tough-love giver, the shoulder to cry on, and so on. If you've ever been on the side that's constantly giving and giving, you know how exhausting and emotionally draining it can be. So, when Beth shared this story with me, I immediately understood why she felt irritated and even like Fay was taking advantage of her.

I also recognized how Beth was able to justify her silent treatment as a response. She knew Fay was vulnerable and didn't want to cause her any more pain. But then Beth took it a step further. She convinced herself that if she were to set firm boundaries with Fay, Fay wouldn't be able to handle it and it would ultimately ruin their friendship. At that point, I couldn't help but point out that I'd prefer boundaries to silence any day of the week, and I think the majority of people would agree.

The truth is that Beth had a habit of attracting this type of dynamic in her life. She often found herself in situations where she would do or give more than she was comfortable with, and then regret it after the fact. Yet, she still continued to give more and more until she reached a breaking point. Once she reached the end of her rope, she still wouldn't assert herself and address the issue. She would just avoid it altogether.

Just as Fay was stuck in a pattern from which she had to break free (by ending her toxic relationship once and for all and focusing on herself), Beth was stuck in her own problematic pattern. She was failing to prioritize her own needs, which often showed up as her inability to establish healthy boundaries.

Beth was stuck in her own story, but at the time she

couldn't see it. So while Fay's narrative may have been that she couldn't be alone, Beth's narrative was that other people's needs took precedence over her own. Even when the dynamic between the two women became too much to handle, Beth still refused to set boundaries with Fay and instead avoided any sort of dialogue. Then she was able to justify her actions by assuming Fay wouldn't be able to handle a conversation about boundaries. She imposed her own storyline onto Fay and thus perpetuated the belief that her own needs weren't important. Rather than establishing healthy boundaries with her friend in an effort to address the false story that her value was determined by her ability to overgive, she perpetuated the cycle.

Don't despair; Beth's story isn't over just yet. In fact, it has a very happy ending. By the time Beth told me about her experience with Fay, several months had passed since that dreary Friday night. In that time, Beth had come to recognize her own narrative and was proactively taking steps to change her story. Hearing her share all the wonderful progress she'd made since the incident got me thinking: How can we get better at recognizing the narrative of our own lives?

In order to transform your story of limitation into one that supports the future you want to create for yourself, consider three key elements:

- Acknowledge the existing narrative

- Become an outside observer
- Choose your next adventure

Acknowledge the Existing Narrative

Most of us are highly skilled at noticing when other people are missing the mark. However, it would be a much better use of our time if we could take that same skill and use it in our own lives to break free from the stories that no longer serve us. Before we can break free from our old story, however, we have to be aware of it.

The key to reaching this awareness can be found within the recurring themes found in your own life. To find them, I suggest you first compile a list of previous experiences that meet all three of the following requirements:

- Recent experiences that resulted in you feeling frustrated, annoyed, or irritated in some way.
- Experiences that you were actively engaged in. In other words, you took part in them and didn't just observe them play out between other people.
- Experiences that felt familiar to you while they were taking place (whether you can or can't put your finger on the exact reason why).

This list doesn't have to be extensive. Once you have anywhere from three to ten experiences on your list, start to look for the patterns woven throughout them. You may be able to find patterns in the way you reacted in the moment, the way you approached the other person involved, the circumstances leading up to the experience, and so forth.

Bring yourself back to these moments in time and become aware of anything that seems reminiscent of other, seemingly unrelated past experiences. For instance, perhaps the people, places, or circumstances in each instance are unique, but the outcome isn't; you've seen it play out time and time again. These patterns and repetitive dynamics are trying to show you or teach you something. Beyond that, you are clinging to a false narrative.

Become an Outside Observer

Once you are aware of the patterns in your own life, you may have everything you need to determine the story that exists underneath it all. However, you may still be uncertain or want some sort of confirmation that you're headed in the right direction. If that's the case, I highly suggest journaling. Journaling has proven to be an effective means to uncover limiting stories. I've found the following journal prompt to be particularly useful in providing breakthroughs and insight into one's story:

What am I avoiding (feeling, experiencing, looking at) in these situations?

It is important to keep the goal of this exercise in mind as you journal using this prompt. You already know the patterns that exist in your life. Now, you're uncovering what these patterns are trying to reveal to you.

During your journaling process, if you find yourself hesitant to delve deeper in a specific direction, that's a good indication that it's exactly where you should explore further. It's natural to gravitate toward the surface-level aspects of your life and the parts of yourself that you already know and with which you're comfortable. But the limiting story underneath it all likely originated from an uncomfortable, negative, or painful experience. In an attempt to keep you "safe" and avoiding future discomfort, your subconscious mind constructed a story that has you stuck playing a role for which you never volunteered. Just like any good storyline, the main character must face some uncomfortable truths and lessons before reaching their next level. Now, it's time to figure out what that story is, even if it's uncomfortable, so you can rewrite it.

If you get stuck or feel like you're getting in your own way for some reason, you may need to take a step back to obtain the clarity you're seeking by creating a bit of space between you and your experiences. By offering yourself a bit of wiggle room, you won't feel as much pressure, which will allow your subconscious mind to be more accessible.

An easy way to establish this space with your journal prompt is to simply create an opening for possibilities through questions and follow-up statements. Using the original journal prompt (What am I avoiding [feeling, experiencing, looking at] in these situations?) as a reference, a corresponding dialogue that creates space would look something like this:

What if I had to guess?

I don't know, but I'm curious about finding out. I might be…

What are some of the potential possibilities?

These follow-up statements and questions don't bind you to anything and remind you that answers aren't necessarily right or wrong, so you can be open to exploring without feeling confined.

If you're still stuck trying to figure out your limiting story, shifting to the perspective of an outside observer will come in handy. As mentioned in Beth's story, it's typically a lot easier to recognize someone else's storyline because as an outside observer, you're able to disconnect emotionally (even if only slightly) so you can see things clearly. You can use this awareness to assist you in the process of uncovering your story of limitations.

As you reflect on your list of life patterns, you may notice particular experiences invoke a stronger emotional reaction than others. Replay one of those experiences in your mind, but this time from the perspective of an outside observer. You can do this through self-hypnosis, visualization, or journaling. What I like to do is visualize myself observing the entire scenario play out as if I'm watching it on television. As I do this exercise, I make a mental note that I am a wise and intuitive observer seeking to understand, rather than pass judgment. In doing so, I can observe myself from an entirely different point of view, almost like I'd watch an actor playing a role. You may discover that as you consider your experiences from a different angle, you're able to hone in on your current story. In the same way, Beth was able to quickly identify Fay's story but not her own.

Choose Your Next Adventure

"At any given moment, you have the power to say: This is not how the story is going to end."

- Christine Mason Miller

Let's pretend that a common theme in your life is extremely contentious breakups. When relationships end, they don't just fizzle out; they explode. Through journaling, you realize that in each one of your relationships that ended in chaos and strife, you did everything you could think of to avoid conflict, to no avail.

As you dig deeper, you realize that what you consider "conflict" other people would most likely call "asserting yourself." By refusing to have a say in your relationships and reframing it as "conflict" in your mind, you inadvertently create a dynamic where you constantly feel unheard and underappreciated.

Naturally, this dynamic isn't sustainable, so eventually the relationship reaches a breaking point. By that time, you have so much resentment built up that you end up lashing out in a highly emotional and destructive manner. While the outburst may make you feel better in the moment, you know you haven't worked through the actual problem, which becomes apparent through the repetitive cycle in which you find yourself. That cycle is a clear indication that you still haven't asserted yourself in a constructive or useful way.

Now that you're fully aware of your limiting story, you have a choice to make. You can continue playing your role in this story of limitation, going in circles and trying to figure out a way to accept the status quo. Or, you can ditch the self-limiting story that you wrote for yourself and become an active participant in creating a new one.

If you're ready to move beyond your old story, then one final step will break you free and create a new one. It all comes down to adopting a new approach, which I like to call, "Choose Your Next Adventure."

Chances are that up until this point, you weren't fully aware of the story you were participating in until after the fact. It's also likely that it wasn't until after the cycle repeated itself that you noticed commonalities. You've essentially been looking back at your story, which makes sense because it's an event that occurred in the past. But as you can imagine, the problem with always looking backward is that you can't see what's right in front of you.

The new approach I suggest you take is much more forward thinking. Instead of reflecting on your story, commit to checking in with yourself through your daily life. To effectively check in, you'll need to have a plan in place; otherwise, you won't actually do it. Using your phone or another electronic device, set three daily alarms. This exercise has no particular time requirement, so space them out to accommodate your schedule. When the alarm goes off, take a moment and check in with yourself. This process can be as simple as asking yourself questions like:

"How am I doing right now?"

"Is this experience aligned with my true story, or am I repeating a cycle?"

"How's my body feeling? Is it trying to tell me something?"

You can pivot anytime you notice yourself going down a path that's not aligned with the future you want for yourself. Armed with this awareness in the moment, you will be able to actively participate in creating a new story for yourself. This approach will take you off autopilot by providing you with daily opportunities to recognize patterns at the conscious level and choose your next adventure whenever necessary.

Several years ago, I recall a friend telling me about a specific book she used to read as a kid. She explained to me that she wasn't a big fan of reading when she was younger, but she really gravitated toward a particular type of book because she felt like an engaged participant in the storyline. I was intrigued by the concept but also somewhat confused, so she explained further. Evidently, these books ended each chapter with a choice for the reader to make. One option led to a different section of the book with a variation of the story. The alternative option led the reader down a different path entirely. Each outcome was different, based on the choice the reader made.

I can't help but recognize the correlation between these books as described by my friend and our own stories. So often, when we have negative experiences with repetitive outcomes, we believe our only recourse is to find a way to accept them. We say things like "it is what it is," as if our experiences are already mapped out for us like a traditional story. But it doesn't have to be this way because you now know the truth. If you don't like the story you're experiencing, you can drop the act, relinquish your role, and actively participate in choosing your next adventure.

CHAPTER 5
DIVE DEEPER

"Trust your unconscious; it knows more than you do."

- Milton H. Erickson, MD

Throughout the course of this book, we've uncovered many truths about the subconscious mind, as well as a variety of methods and exercises you can use to improve your life at the subconscious level.

Without this knowledge, many people walk through life believing their conscious mind is running the show. It makes sense that they would arrive at this conclusion because the conscious mind does seem to be at the forefront. Without having all the facts, one would assume that's where the power resides. But as you know, that's not typically the case. In fact, your subconscious mind has a much greater impact on your overall life experience. So, although your subconscious may seem to linger unassumingly in the background of your daily life for the most part, you shouldn't dismiss it.

Past, Present, Future

I'm fairly certain we can all agree on one truth, which is that no two people are exactly alike on every single level. Every human is a unique individual with a distinctive personality, varying interests, and life experiences. Even twins who are raised in the same household, wear the same clothes, and experience similar life events perceive and interpret their lives differently. Of course, that's not to dismiss the notion that you'll always find people who feel familiar or remind you of someone else you know, even if you can't put your finger on exactly why. In a similar sense, groups of people often behave similarly according to the environment in which they were raised. Still, these similarities do not detract from our individual identities. At the end of the day, you are uniquely you and I am uniquely me.

Keeping that in mind, I'd like you to take a moment and think about the many relationships you've had throughout your life and all the individuals you've met along the way. You don't need to go down any emotional rabbit holes for this exercise or dive too deep into a particular relationship. Almost as if you're taking inventory in your mind, think about your past coworkers, romantic partners, childhood friends, roommates, close family members, distant relatives, and even the people you see in passing and consider acquaintances. Go ahead and close your eyes and focus on the variety of people you've met throughout your life experience thus far.

Once you've completed your mental inventory rundown, I'd like you to consider this: Throughout your lifetime, you've associated with a wide range of people and formed a variety of relationships, as verified by the mental exercise you just completed. Even if you've never left your hometown, you work from home, and/or you typically prefer to keep your social circle small, this fact will still ring true for you.

As you reflect on the conversations and interactions you've had with individuals from all walks of life, you will undoubtedly notice many stark differences. One of the very obvious differences will be that some people are incredibly future-focused; the future is all they think about. Others are so stuck in the past that it seems almost as if they're living there. Only a select few live in the present moment.

Ideally, we would all be living in the present moment. In doing so, we would alleviate much of the anxiety associated with the future's uncertainty. Additionally, if we were more present, we could significantly reduce lingering feelings of sadness and despair that are associated with living in the past.

If you've ever tried to shift your focus from one end of the spectrum (either the past or the future) to the center (the present moment), you know it's a daunting task that requires constant redirecting. In fact, this is one of the rare instances where it's actually easier to make the mental shift from one extreme to the other (living in the past to pining for the future, for instance), instead of stopping halfway and trying to stay in the present moment.

When faced with this challenge, the masses often advise meditation. While I'm a big believer in the benefits of meditation, I'm also well aware that telling someone to "start meditating" isn't very helpful when they're overwhelmed with constant thoughts about the past or future. Plus, meditating can be surprisingly difficult, especially when you're first starting out. Let's face it—although it isn't a complicated process, it requires your full commitment in the moment, in terms of both time and effort. Sometimes, you just want to take action, or at the very least know you're making progress towards your goal. For many people, meditation doesn't satisfy that need.

As I previously stated, in an ideal world, we would all live in the present moment and in a constant state of peace and harmony ... but that's not real life. Real life is messy. Although you might be generally more past or future-focused, you're still juggling your current experiences, memories from your past, and thoughts about your future, at least to some extent.

With that said, as you make your way through the remaining sections of this book, you'll learn how your memories can help you reframe past experiences that keep you stuck in a loop. Additionally, you'll learn how to use your dreams to better understand your current experience. These key techniques will allow you to feel more at ease with living in the past or future, as you work your way toward a more present mindset.

Understanding Your Memory

Since you've made it to this point in the book, I'm confident you're well-versed in many of the key takeaways surrounding the subconscious mind. As you may recall, your habits, beliefs, and emotions reside within your subconscious mind. However, we have yet to explore one aspect of your inner mind. Contained within your subconscious mind are also your long-term memories.

Generally, we tend to trust that our memories are a true and valid representation of our past experiences. However, if you've ever watched a childhood home video of yourself, perhaps at a birthday party or family reunion, you may notice that at least some discrepancies exist between the memories you have of the experience and the actual video of it. Clearly, our memories waver in precision.

Knowing that the subconscious mind accepts what it's given at face value and doesn't particularly read between the lines, you might also believe that once you experience a memorable moment, your memory of that experience is locked in your subconscious mind. You may even go so far as to think that your memories are etched in stone, so to speak. But as you will soon discover, that's not necessarily the case.

As you gain a newfound awareness about your memory, you may find it opens the door to more questions. You may even begin to question your own memories and doubt yourself. After all, if you can't trust your own memories, what/who can you trust? But before you start down the path of questioning your entire existence, I want you to be aware that this knowledge can actually be very useful to you. As you continue to understand key features of your memory, you can learn how to make peace with your past, and as a result, create a more promising future. For example, by learning how to take an old memory that stifled you as a child and soften it up a bit, you can create a more positive outcome in your next chapter.

As we explore the many facets of your memory, including memory retrieval and memory malleability, you will see how this knowledge can afford you multiple opportunities to rewrite aspects of your past that hold you back from creating the future you want and rightfully deserve.

Memory Retrieval

The way memory functions kind of reminds me of a long-term parking garage at an airport, with each vehicle parked in the garage representing a different memory. On the other side of the airport is the short-term parking for quick trips and fast drop-off/pick-up exchanges. Naturally, this section makes me think of our conscious mind and all the fleeting thoughts we have as we navigate through our daily lives and recent experiences.

One might think that between the two different parking areas, short-term parking (the conscious mind) would have more turnover, and that's a pretty accurate assumption. We make conscious decisions continuously throughout the day and take action based on our conscious reasoning and observations. The conscious mind sees a lot of movement, and for the most part, it evolves and changes pretty regularly, as you would probably expect.

But back in long-term parking (the subconscious mind), it's a whole different scenario. The long-term parking vehicles are much more likely to remain parked in the garage for an extended period of time, although not forever. Similarly, our subconscious stores long term (and sometimes lifelong) aspects of who we are and what we're all about. This storage includes past experiences that influence our actions and behaviors in our present reality. In other words, this part of our brains is where our memories are located.

Having had many different experiences throughout our lives, we obviously have countless memories stored within our subconscious minds. From time to time and for a variety of reasons, we retrieve a memory from our past, which is what it means to "remember." The process of retrieving a memory is comparable to driving your car out of the long-term parking garage. Your memories, just like the cars, will eventually make their way to the front at some point.

What happens when they do make their way to the forefront is ultimately very surprising. Many people are shocked to discover the truth about what really happens when you call up a memory. Every time you go to retrieve a memory from your past, you're literally re-membering. What I mean by that is you're not remembering the original event from the same perspective you had when you experienced it. What you're genuinely remembering is your most recent memory of the original memory.

Let's say you're reminiscing about your childhood and you remember a time when you received a stuffed animal as a gift for your seventh birthday. This is one of your favorite childhood memories, so you often revisit it over the years. But when you retrieve the memory, you're not remembering it from the perspective of the seven-year-old version of you in that moment. You're remembering the version of that memory that exists from the last time you remembered it.

On its own, this insight isn't too significant in terms of how it affects your relationship with your memories, but it becomes noteworthy when you realize that each time you revisit a memory, it will manifest subtle changes. These changes are especially prevalent in the insignificant aspects of the memory and the things you deem inconsequential, like perhaps the color of the living room rug.

Why does this susceptibility to change even matter? Well, the way you perceive a memory the most recent time you remember it sets the stage for you to feel either empowered and strong or weak and insignificant because when you retrieve a memory, you open the door to potentially place your current mental and emotional state into that memory. The degree to which your memory is affected depends on your memory malleability at that time.

Memory Malleability

Did you catch the part where I slipped in the word 'malleable' in regard to memory? I was really surprised by that revelation when I learned it. Things are not always as they seem, and this adage rings especially true when it comes to the different aspects and inner workings of the mind. Contrary to popular belief, your memories aren't concrete; they are in fact malleable, regardless of whether or not you think you have an excellent memory. So, whether you remember everything and think you have the memory of an elephant or you can barely remember what you ate for dinner last night doesn't have any bearing on your existing memories and their malleability.

Our memories' malleability is a lot like absurdly tall, thin palm trees that sway in the wind. On cloudless days, in a subtle breeze, they sway from side to side ever so slightly. But then the days come when the weather is more intense and the winds blow fiercely. The trees flop back and forth from one side to the other and look like they will almost certainly snap in half at some point. However, they almost never break. Their level of pliability is dependent on the wind's intensity.

In a similar manner, the extent to which our memories are malleable is dependent on specific conditions. When you recall a memory through sensory as opposed to abstract details, the memory becomes extremely pliable. In that state, the memory is reprogrammable. Just as the palm trees reveal their flexibility when they meet certain conditions (like strong winds), your memories reveal their malleability when they meet certain factors that reopen the memory, making it available to reprogram. The key is the sensory details.

reprogramming memories — software upgrade

Once you retrieve the memory through sensory details, you have six hours during which that memory is susceptible to change. You will either perceive this time limit as good or bad news, depending on how you utilize this information.

Let's start with the bad-news scenario. Having six hours with your memory in a malleable state might be bad news if what you experience during that time (including your thoughts, feelings, and mindset) has a negative impact on your memory. For instance, if you're in a bad mood or feeling sad and exhausted, then those feelings are going to assimilate into that memory.

But here's the good news: Because your memory is malleable for six hours, you have an extensive amount of time to create alternative memories. Doing so will soften up past memories, and in some ways allow you to rewrite the past. While the sequence of events won't necessarily change, your perception and the way you feel about the memory can. This fact is especially useful in moving beyond painful memories.

Keep in mind that as you reopen your memory and make it susceptible to new perceptions, you're giving your emotional state, feelings, and mindset the power to sway that memory. During that span of six hours, it's important that you're aware of what's going on in your inner world so you can manage it accordingly.

If our present emotions are extreme on one end of the spectrum and we retrieve a memory with opposing emotions, then we have essentially opened the door and welcomed in our present emotions to impact the existing memory. The extent to which our memory is altered is based on how malleable a state our memory is in and the difference between your current state and the existing memory. If it's vastly different, then expect your memory to sway, just like palm trees do in harsh winds.

When you remember a memory, if changes occur to that memory, those changes will stick. Then, the next time you go to remember that same memory, those changes will be reflected in that experience. So, as you might imagine, remembering a memory doesn't just bring you back to that experience emotionally; it also brings your current emotions and feelings into the memory.

A Positive Perception of the Past

Knowing that your memories are malleable might lead you to question your past, but that's not necessarily a bad thing. The advantage of having this awareness is that you can alter your negative perception of old memories, or at the very least make reflecting on them more bearable. You can find great comfort in knowing that if you have a negative experience in life, you can have somewhat of a "redo" in terms of how you perceive that memory. The method to accomplish this reboot is through softening traumatic memories that impacted your life in a negative way. By essentially "taking the sting out" of a memory, you neutralize a significant amount of the pain associated with it. As a result, the life experiences that were once adversely affected by the memory will become significantly easier.

To soften a traumatic memory, you'll first need to make sure you're in a good emotional and mental state. The first step is to check in with yourself. If you're having a particularly good day without a worry in the world, then you should be good to go. If you're not feeling that way right off the bat, then you'll need to make an effort to get into a positive space, both mentally and emotionally, before revisiting the past memory.

You can accomplish this feat in a number of ways.

You might already have a process or method you rely on to get into a positive headspace, but if not, I would suggest a physiological approach in combination with positive affirmations. The physical piece could be as simple as going on a brisk walk out in nature or taking a hot shower. The goal is to change your current physical state, and in doing so, your mood should adjust accordingly.

I'm sure you know how challenging it can be to overcome a bad mood or a negative mindset. Whether it's the result of a particularly rough day or you have no valid explanation for why you're feeling down, the truth remains: Pulling yourself out of a funk isn't easy. I've often found that the harder we try to make ourselves feel better, the worse we end up feeling. I believe the reasoning for this paradox is twofold.

First, when we judge ourselves (as revealed through our non-acceptance of our current mood), our subconscious mind seems to almost double down on its stance. Fortunately, if you find yourself in this situation, you can resolve it fairly easily. In order to release the harsh judgment of your current mood, you need to accept it before you can comfortably and successfully move beyond it. Now, accepting it doesn't mean that you enjoy being in a bad mood or that you agree to continue with a negative mindset. Instead, accepting your current state is all about feeling your feelings without resistance. A great way to do this exercise is to imagine your negative feelings or mindset as a color that flows through your body and then exits through the bottom of your feet.

Using myself as an example, here's how this exercise would look. Let's pretend for a moment that I'm in a terrible mood and I need to work through it quickly. I know from experience that telling myself to "think positive thoughts" isn't going to cut it. I lie down and close my eyes (which is really difficult because I'm stressed and annoyed). At this point, I have a tension headache, so I visualize the stress that I'm feeling due to my mood as a red hue. In my mind's eye, I picture this red hue starting at the top of my head and slowly moving throughout my body. I feel all my feelings as I do this, knowing that they will pass. Rather than visualizing the red hue that represents my tension and bad mood coating my body from head to toe, I visualize it moving through my body without leaving any trace behind. Once it reaches the bottom of my feet, it dissolves completely. Now that I have accepted those feelings rather than resisting them, I'm much more capable of moving past them.

Beyond accepting our current state, there's another reason I believe we often feel worse when we try to pull ourselves out of a bad mood. It all comes down to the approach we take. You see, from a practical standpoint, it makes perfect sense that if you're not in the best mood, the way to resolve it would be through reason and understanding. So, you might try to turn your mood around through words of encouragement. When that doesn't work, you might try a more aggressive tactic (still based on logic and reason). That might look like a "tough love" approach or making forceful demands of yourself. Still, despite your best efforts, your mood doesn't shift.

At this point, you've put forth an extensive effort to feel better without success. But the truth is, you don't have to approach this problem from an intellectual, practical, or even logical angle. Many physiological approaches are far easier, more efficient, and much more effective at improving your mental state.

Over the years, I've discovered a number of physiological approaches that I've used to temporarily change my physical state very quickly (sometimes even instantly), and as a result, my mood and mindset have improved significantly. These approaches are as follows:

- Blast cold air on your face. (This method is especially effective if you're in your car and need a quick pick-me-up. Just be sure to park your car before you attempt it.)
- Take a cold shower. I know it sounds miserable (and it will be for a brief moment), but oddly

enough, it's highly effective, even if it's just a 30-second quick rinse in cold water.

- Jump around. Perhaps it's due to the childhood memories that jumping elicits or simply the increased heart rate, but either way, find a way to jump around! Do 50 jumping jacks, jump on a mini-trampoline for 60 seconds, or simply jump in place.
- Change your scenery. Spending time in nature is one of my favorite ways to improve my mood and mental state. It can also be very grounding too, which is certainly a welcome bonus.

Once you're in a positive mental and emotional state, you can begin the process of revisiting the painful memory by visualizing, simply re-imagining the experience in your mind's eye, or with the support of a hypnotherapist. As you revisit the memory, be sure to focus on sensory details. In doing so, you'll re-open it. From that point forward and for the next six hours, your positive emotional state, feelings, and mindset will intermingle with the memory. This state of affairs might not change your overall memory in terms of the experience itself, but it will soften the pain associated with it.

In the future, when you revisit that memory you will be revisiting it as you experienced it the last time you remembered it, so the positive state you were in at the time will now be part of that memory. As a result of softening the memory, much of the power it once had over you will subside, which will empower you to make peace with your past and move forward.

Memory Reconstruction

Since your memory is malleable, you are capable of not only swaying how you feel about a memory, but rewriting history (at least in your own mind). You can literally change the outcome of your past experiences in your mind and convince your subconscious mind that you're limitless. You truly do have the ability to alter the way you remember events from the past.

If this feels too good to be true, I want you to remember that if you can convince yourself that "this is how it's always been, so this is how it will always be," then you can also convince yourself of a new story that aligns with the future you dream about living.

Please understand that interlacing a more positive perception on an existing memory and literally reconstructing a memory are two entirely different things. While in theory it might be a nice idea to reconstruct the past to find relief from anxiety, stress, and other negative feelings, it's not something we can do at will. Sure, it can happen from time to time, but when it does, it's not intentional. However, when it comes to placing an alternate spin or perception on a memory, we can do so—both intentionally and unintentionally.

For instance, I had a client named Lenny who came to see me for help with her dating life. She felt like she had some sort of subconscious block and found herself constantly ignoring red flags in the men she dated. It wasn't until her relationships became so bad and the red flags became so obvious and numerous that she would finally admit to herself, "Hey, this might not be the guy for me."

She would meet a new guy and notice a potential issue right off the bat, but then dismiss it. At some point, months down the line, her friends would meet her new romantic interest. Time and again, they would notice a handful of red flags and relay that information to Lenny. Now, you might think that if Lenny was ignoring these red flags then she must not have wanted to see them, and her friends should back off or at the very least keep it to themselves, as she clearly didn't care.

Even so, Lenny wasn't upset with her friends' commentary because they were continuously proven right. As her relationships progressed, Lenny would eventually have a revelation similar to her friends' insights and dump the guy. She couldn't help wondering, "Why are my friends so good at recognizing these red flags and I'm not?"

As it turns out, Lenny constantly distorted scenarios in her mind when it came to her relationships with men, which allowed her to overlook the glaringly obvious red flags that were right in front of her. She softened the initial experience by reframing not only her perception of it, but the actual experience itself.

When I asked for an example of her dating history, she told me about a guy named Jeff who she'd dated the year prior. After a few weeks of dating, the two of them went out to dinner and Jeff spent the entire meal scrolling through his ex-girlfriend's social media accounts and talking about it to his buddies through text. This behavior went on for hours.

After she got home, Lenny texted her friends a recap of her date in which she had nothing nice to say about him. Jeff's actions were not only wildly inappropriate on many levels, but also very bizarre. To say Lenny was upset would be an understatement. Her number one pet peeve is rude behavior, followed by people who ignore her. After that date, Lenny said, "Jeff looked like a huge red flag flapping in the wind."

As you might imagine, her friends were surprised when she brought him to a get-together a couple of weeks later. One of her friends pulled her aside to ask about the situation and Lenny recanted, "Oh, I was just overreacting. He wasn't on his phone the whole time, he was just checking in with work."

However, that version wasn't true. Although it may seem like Lenny was clearly covering for Jeff because she liked him, that wasn't the case either. She truly believed her new narrative because it's what she 'remembered' had happened. It's not uncommon for people to revise history to align with their wants and needs; yet it can be pretty disorienting to realize that you can create false memories and actually believe that something happened when it never really occurred.

So what exactly happened here? Did Lenny go home after her date with Jeff, light a candle, close her eyes, and commit to revising the memory of her red-flag-filled date? Absolutely not.

I believe what happened is that after some time, Jeff brought up the memory when Lenny was in a particularly good mood. He either deliberately or unknowingly provided a lot of sensory details of the night with an "updated" version of what happened. This, paired with the fact that Lenny wanted to ignore the red flags and was in a good emotional state, shifted her perception. Time passed, and when she went to revisit the memory again, she wasn't returning to the initial event but the memory of the event. So, when she went to retrieve her memory the next time, her mind reconstructed it, pulling now from a jumble of information.

When retrieving and recalling past experiences, our subconscious mind has an abundance of information with which to work, which is especially true if we're constantly recalling the same memories over and over again. These "frequently visited" memories are more susceptible to becoming convoluted simply because they have more opportunities to be exposed to an excess of information.

Before our subconscious mind retrieves a memory from our past experiences, it reconstructs it. When it does this, it's not just pulling from the experience or the last time you remembered it.

Included in the reconstruction of your memory is:

- The memory itself
- Your perception of the memory the last time you remembered it
- Your emotions at that time
- The way you feel and your overall mood
- Your current attitude and knowledge

Although Lenny was initially very clear about what took place during her date with Jeff, at some point in her memory recall, her recollection became distorted. Not only was she unable to accurately recall her initial negative feelings about her experience, but her memories were distorted by her current, more favorable feelings towards Jeff.

Avoid Distorted Memories

While having the ability to distort the way we perceive our past experiences can certainly be beneficial in some situations, it's not always the best option. Sometimes we want to remember our past exactly as we experienced it because it was such a beautiful moment. Other experiences may not be as enjoyable to remember, but we need to keep them intact in order to protect the ones we love, stand up for ourselves, or ultimately make the right decisions as we move forward in our lives.

Knowing all the variables and the slew of information that's constantly surrounding each memory can feel slightly overwhelming. It can almost feel like the only way to avoid distorting your memories is to stop retrieving them. However, you can take some measures to minimize heavily-distorted memories.

One option is to be very deliberate about your experience when you recall a memory. Take an inventory of sorts beforehand, if possible. Check your mood, your mindset, any recurring thoughts or themes (if they exist), your intention for retrieval, and anything else you deem relevant or potentially significant. When doing this, if you realize that you're not in a very patient mood, then you can make the judgment call to shift your focus before moving forward to retrieve memories of the past. While it may seem very simple, doing this quick rundown to check in with yourself first will allow you to maintain your memory without major distortions.

Another strategy to overcome your inclination to distort memories is to compartmentalize your emotions and thoughts prior to retrieval. You can accomplish this end in many ways, but I particularly like this simple visualization process:

1. Visualize yourself in a white room. One of the walls is lined with cardboard filing boxes. Little pieces of paper are scattered about on the floor. Each paper reveals an emotion, thought, or feeling that you're experiencing.
2. Visualize yourself picking up one piece of paper at a time, reading the word that's written on it, processing that emotion, and then placing it in a box and putting a lid on it. Continue to do this exercise until no papers are left on the floor.
3. Remind yourself that the contents of each box (every emotion, thought, and feeling) will remain there until you're ready to access them again.
4. The final step is to visualize yourself leaving the room, knowing that you've accomplished your goal of compartmentalizing your emotions and thoughts prior to retrieving your memory.

The last tactic I have to share with you is what Lenny unintentionally did during her experience. If you have a memory you are concerned may become distorted, consider consulting with other people who were present when the actual event occurred. Or, relay the information and context to an outside party (ideally, a friend who tends to retain information well or truly listens). Another alternative would be to write down the experience so you have it as a frame of reference down the line.

Each of these options can provide you with more accountability than you can provide yourself. While no solutions are guaranteed, these strategies only take a couple of minutes to implement, and at the very least they will provide you with a protective barrier between your memories and future distortions.

Dream Therapy

"Man is a genius when he is dreaming."

- Akira Kurosawa

The subconscious mind is fascinating on many levels, but of all its unique traits and features (and as you've learned, it has many), I believe our dreams reign supreme. The dreams we have, especially those we remember after the fact, have significant meaning. No matter how bizarre or outlandish they may seem, something of value can be found within each of them.

Naturally, to find the meaning, you must be willing to look. But as you may know, interpreting our dreams can often feel very "hit or miss" because sometimes the things our subconscious mind comes up with don't seem to make any sense—at least not from a logical perspective.

Our dreams are the language of our subconscious mind. They are the way our subconscious tries to communicate with us. But just like any mutually beneficial relationship, communication is a two-way street, and to truly appreciate the significance that can be found in each dream, you have to be willing to listen to what your subconscious mind is trying to tell you.

Dreams speak to us in two different ways. Each and every thing you experience in your dream can be broken up and divided into one of these two categories:

- Literal
- Symbolic

Often, our dreams feel real when we experience them, sometimes even hours and days later. This feeling of reality makes sense when we have a dream that's fairly literal. One could assume that literal dreams feel real because, well, they're realistic. It's not completely out of the realm of possibility that a strikingly similar experience could occur in real life. So what about the strange and outrageous dreams that either don't make any sense whatsoever or are so wildly imaginative that they could never occur in real life? What I find to be even more fascinating than these dreams themselves is that oftentimes they feel just as real, if not more real, than the most realistic dreams.

Behind every "this could never happen in real life" dream is a wealth of symbolic meaning. So, rather than writing these dreams off as being very peculiar or too hard to interpret, get curious about them. I assure you that if you're willing to explore the symbolic meaning within your dreams, you'll be very happy you did. By gaining a thorough understanding of how to interpret your dreams, you may find that you're able to mentally work through issues from your past, gain a better understanding of your underlying feelings, and show up better prepared for future life experiences.

If you have ever read a dream interpretation book or searched for something along the lines of, "What does it mean when you dream about…" in your web browser, then you're likely aware of how confusing and frankly unhelpful most of the information available on dream analysis is. That's because a lot of these resources focus on static dream symbols. Their content is based on the assumption that each symbolic meaning within a dream has the same meaning across the board for every individual, but that's not always the case.

For instance, if I have a dream that involves a bird flying in the sky, a static dream interpretation might tell me that the bird symbolizes freedom, and maybe it does symbolize that for some people. But the context really matters too, which is not taken into consideration under the assumption that symbols are one-size-fits-all. What if, at some point in my personal life experience, I had a pet bird who got out of his cage and flew away? One cannot reasonably assume that my feelings surrounding that personal experience wouldn't impact my feelings towards the symbolism of a bird. Therefore, the bird in my dream could symbolize something other than this static interpretation. My subconscious may not be trying to convey freedom or anything of the sort through a dream with a bird flying away. The bird could symbolize being left behind or losing something I once loved dearly.

Rather than relying on someone else to be the expert in the interpretation of your dreams, I'm going to share a technique with you that will provide you with the tools to be your own dream interpreter. At the end of the day, no one is going to be able to uncover the symbolic meaning behind your dreams better than you—the person experiencing the dream firsthand.

Dream Stages

The sleep cycle has five stages, and within those stages are the three stages of the dream cycle. The three stages of dreams are: 1) wishful thinking, 2) precognitive, and 3) venting. While our focus is going to be primarily on the venting stage, it's important to have a brief understanding of each cycle for reference.

Within the first two hours of the sleep cycle, you enter the wishful thinking stage. In this stage, the mind does an inventory of the experiences and thoughts that occurred throughout the day and decides what is important enough to keep for later and what to discard.

The next stage of dreaming is the precognitive stage. During this stage, your subconscious mind compiles and filters through your past experiences with the additional information that it received during the day. It uses this insight to attempt to predict your future.

The final stage (and most important in terms of dream interpretation), is the venting stage. Throughout the day, your mind has acquired an overload of information. At this stage in the dream cycle, your mind attempts to release the excess. In order to accomplish this task, you must fulfill two requirements on your end. The first is that you must be ready to let go of what you've been holding on to. The second is that while in the dream state, you can feel the dream through your senses. In doing so, you can safely and somewhat comfortably embrace heavy and intense emotions, such as fear, without judgment.

Remember Your Dreams

When you wake up after a long night's sleep and remember your dream, that dream likely occurred during the venting stage. However, some people tend to remember their dreams more often than others. If you struggle to remember your dreams, you're going to have a hard time interpreting them. If you fall into this category, you can follow this simple practice and develop the habit of remembering your dreams.

1. Before you head to bed tonight, take a sheet of blank paper and fold it into fourths just like you would if you were making a homemade card. (First, fold it in half lengthwise and then in half widthwise.)
2. Open the paper back up and inside write, "I'm going to have a venting dream tonight to release my fears/concerns/frustrations around…" and add your goal to the end of the sentence.
3. Fold the paper back the way you had it and write, "Remember to remember your dreams" on the front of it before you place it on your

nightstand or somewhere next to your bed.

4. Before you go to sleep and when you wake up in the morning, you'll see this paper, and it will serve as a reminder.
5. Each morning, write down your dream in as much detail as possible. This should be your very first task of the day.
6. Commit to doing the following practice for the next 21 days. Doing so will help you develop the habit of remembering your dreams, and as a result, you will begin to remember more of them.

Love it!

Dream Analysis Process

The process of interpreting your dreams is fairly straightforward and far more helpful (in my opinion) than a static dream analysis. Rather than attempting to do this exercise in your head, I highly suggest you write it out in the exact manner I'll describe. Not only will this method help you "see" all the different aspects of your dream, but writing it out creates space between you and your dream. This space is essential, as you will be analyzing symbolic messages that hold a lot of meaning to you at a subconscious level. As we've discussed at length, sometimes it's difficult to analyze our own experiences as effectively as we analyze others' experiences.

So, the distance that putting pen to paper creates is ideal.

Ready to determine what your subconscious mind is trying to tell you through your dreams? Simply make a T chart on a piece of paper and label the left side "literal" and the right side "symbolic." Reflect on the dream you had and divide all the key elements into one section or the other, regardless of whether it makes sense or not. The literal side is where you will put everything that has happened to you in real life or makes sense because it resonates with you on some literal level. The symbolic side will be much more extensive—that's where you'll put all the strange or seemingly meaningless aspects of the dream; basically, it's where all the stuff that doesn't make a ton of sense goes.

When you've finished, take a step back and see if you can understand what your subconscious mind was trying to communicate with you. The literal side doesn't require interpretation. Therefore, start with that side as a reference to determine a bit of what the dream was about. Then, as you make your way to the symbolic side, you have to start asking yourself questions to uncover the true meaning of each symbol. Some examples of these types of questions include:

- What is the relationship between the symbolic aspects of your dream and your present life?
- What emotions does each symbol evoke?

- What effect did it have on you? Why?
- How did it make you feel?

Here's an example of what this process might look like. Imagine for a moment that you are a college student and you work at a restaurant part-time. The restaurant is not your priority, as your studies often take precedence. But during the summer, things are a bit different. You spend a lot of time working—much more than usual. Before you know it, the fall semester is starting and you forget to cut back your hours at the restaurant. So, a couple of weeks go by during which you work full time and go to school full time, and it's a lot to juggle. Financially, you don't need to do this to yourself. After a few weeks of overworking, you decide that rather than burning yourself out, you'll start giving away your shifts, which is completely fine with your manager.

Then, in the middle of all of this commotion, you have a dream that wakes you up in the night. In this dream, you haven't worked at the restaurant in nearly three years and suddenly, out of nowhere, you have your job back for whatever reason. It's a very busy evening and you're in full-fledged panic mode because you don't remember your code to get into the computer to take the orders. To make matters worse, you don't know the table numbers, so you have no idea where your section even is or who your customers are. Oh, and that's not it! You're also doing everything, from washing the dishes to making the salads in the kitchen. Then suddenly everything goes black in the restaurant. The lights shut off, the electricity goes out, and a giant creature, like some sort of elephant, comes through the front door and the entire building collapses.

As you think about this dream, it's fairly easy to pick up on the literal context. For instance, you know that you've been very busy. You've been feeling overworked, and you've been working at a restaurant, so this part of the dream feels pretty relevant to what you're currently experiencing. But that's where the similarities between your dream and your real life would appear to end. Obviously, no elephants are walking through the door, the building hasn't collapsed as far as you know, and you're working less, not more.

While many symbols are woven into this dream, let's focus on the two big ones: the elephant and the building collapsing. As you start asking yourself some questions that are relevant to the symbols above, you can't help but wonder what the elephant walking in the room could represent. Something big is going on in your life that you are consciously ignoring, but your subconscious definitely isn't. Given the fact that you were overwhelmed doing so many jobs and the job you were hired to do was the one you struggled with the most, you might conclude that you felt taken advantage of and stretched way too thin in that position. The building collapsing could symbolize your fear that you couldn't keep it all together and that everything was going to fall apart if something didn't change.

Typically, our dreams aren't overly literal. If they were, then we wouldn't really feel the need to analyze them. The symbolism that weaves into our dreams sparks an innate curiosity within us, compelling us to want to know more. By analyzing the symbolic meaning of our dreams, we essentially build a bridge between the excess information our subconscious is ready to release (or vent out) and our conscious awareness. This metaphorical bridge allows us to better understand ourselves, as well as recognize the patterns within our lives that we may have otherwise overlooked. As a result, we can uncover information about ourselves and our lives that we may have not consciously recognized previously. Our dream analysis can reveal many things to us, including clues concerning where we should put more of our focus and which areas of our lives we need to improve.

As you can tell, uncovering the underlying meaning of your dreams has many benefits, so don't be afraid to get curious and poke around a bit in order to uncover what your subconscious mind is trying to tell you. Using the methods described above to interpret the symbols within your dreams, you can experience a much more fulfilling existence through a newfound understanding of who you are and the life you lead.

With that being said, it's important to keep in mind that it is possible to over-analyze your dreams and derail all of your efforts as a result. Excessive analysis of the symbols in your dreams can put the information your brain was trying to vent out right back into your subconscious mind. So, while you had the dream when you had it for a reason, and it certainly wasn't random, try not to force meaning where you can't find it.

A general rule of thumb to avoid over-analyzing your dreams is to simply follow the dream analysis process as described previously and check in with yourself throughout the process. During your self check-in, if you notice any of the following red flags, you should press pause on your dream analysis. Here are some signs you're overdoing it:

- You're extensively searching for meaning in every minor detail of the dream to no avail.
- Somewhere along the line you unintentionally went rogue and you're no longer following the dream analysis process.
- You're forcing meaning onto the symbols in your dreams regardless of whether they sit right with you. You're determined to make everything mean something.
- Your dream analysis doesn't come easily to you or "flow" in any way. It's a stressful, time-consuming experience.

If any of these red flags pop up as you check in with yourself throughout your analysis, you have a couple of options to move forward. You can pause your analysis, take a break, and revisit the dream at a better time (like when you're in a calmer state of mind or feel more clear-headed). Another option (which is especially helpful if your overanalysis is due to a specific, particularly mind-boggling dream) is to abandon your analysis, especially if it's causing you unnecessary stress or you feel like you're digging for meaning but keep coming up empty.

Now, you may interpret this advice as me suggesting you "give up," but if that's your take on it, please humor me and consider an alternative perspective. As I mentioned previously, it's possible to take the information your subconscious mind was trying to vent out and unintentionally put it right back into your subconscious mind. A common way this issue can occur is through over-analyzing your dreams. So, in situations where this outcome is possible, it's better to stop your analysis and allow your subconscious to eliminate the excess, rather than hand-delivering the excess information back to your subconscious mind.

In general, however, as long as you follow the dream analysis process and commit to check in with yourself throughout the process, the pros of analyzing your dreams far surpass the cons. If you're ever in a situation where you're overdoing it, you will likely be well aware of it and be able to adjust accordingly before it negatively impacts your experience.

Self Mastery

Undoubtedly, your subconscious mind plays an important role in your life experiences. It has many functions, from storing your habits and beliefs to trying to keep you safe and attempting to communicate with you through your dreams. While everyone has access to their subconscious mind, not everyone utilizes it to its full potential. I don't believe this tendency is due to disinterest or general unwillingness, but rather a lack of understanding around the inner mind's workings.

In the past, you may have allowed your subconscious mind to linger in the background of your life, completely unaware that it was running the show. Perhaps you tried to strong-arm your way through bad habits, relying solely on willpower. Maybe you pushed your own story of limitation onto your friends in an attempt to protect them from making the same mistakes you did. It's possible you made all of your big life decisions based solely on logic and never explored your intuitive side. Maybe you even wrongly assumed that your vivid and bizarre dreams were meaningless or dismissed them as "just your imagination."

Whether you started this book in hopes of learning more about the subconscious mind, the power of hypnotherapy, or how to experience more success, my hope is that it opened your eyes to the unlimited power you have within to create an exceptional life for yourself.

You now have the tools to break free from outdated habits that hinder your growth and prevent you from stepping into who you are truly meant to be. My wish is that you feel both empowered and curious to continue diving deeper, looking within, and exploring all the different facets of your subconscious mind.

As you navigate through life armed with the strategies outlined in this book, I encourage you to continue pursuing new, creative ways to bridge the gap between your outward experience and the inner workings of your subconscious mind. Having the ability to guide your inner mind toward your goals and dreams will not only help you achieve them faster, but it will also allow you to do so with less stress, more focus, and an even greater sense of purpose.

REFERENCES

Professional Hypnotism Manual, John G. Kappas, Ph.D. 7th Edition 2015

University of Colorado at Boulder. (2018, December 10). Your brain on imagination: It's a lot like reality, study shows. ScienceDaily. Retrieved October 13, 2021 from
www.sciencedaily.com/releases/2018/12/181210144943.htm

→ being a storyteller
  ↳ recalling facts → telling eloquent stories
→ healthy postive
→ embodying the spiritual warrior
→ making the most of my time in gov
→ singing
→ partnering w/ my equal (reprogram beliefs about love)
→ becoming the 1% through providing good jobs
→ being a phenomenal connector/networker
→ fix hiring
→ Reach out to Christian
Ask Chat GP4?